CHILDREN

Nicola Madge

First published in Great Britain in February 2006 by

The Policy Press
University of Bristol
Fourth Floor, Beacon House
Queen's Road
Clifton
Bristol BS8 1QU
UK

Tel +44 (0)117 331 4054
Fax +44 (0)117 331 4093
e-mail tpp-info@bristol.ac.uk
www.policypress.org.uk

© Nicola Madge 2006

British Library Cataloguing in Publication Data
A catalogue record for this book is available from the British Library.

Library of Congress Cataloging-in-Publication Data
A catalog record for this book has been requested.

ISBN-10 1 86134 783 9 paperback
ISBN-13 978 1 86134 783 1

A hardcover version of this book is also available

Nicola Madge is Assistant Research Director at the National Children's Bureau (NCB). NCB promotes the voices, interests and well-being of all children and young people across every aspect of their lives. As an umbrella body for the children's sector in England and Northern Ireland, it provides essential information on policy, research and best practice for members and other partners. More at www.ncb.org.uk

Cover design by Qube Design Associates, Bristol.
Front cover: photograph supplied by kind permission of Getty Images.
Printed and bound in Great Britain by Hobbs the Printers, Southampton.

Contents

List of tables and figures

Tables

Figures

Acknowledgements

Two thousand children and young people, as well as more than five hundred adults, gave their views on the meaning of childhood these days. My thanks go, first and foremost, to everyone who told it as it is.

It takes organisation to carry out a research study and I would like to acknowledge the help and enthusiasm received in undertaking the surveys. First, a very big thank you to all the schools that cooperated in the study, as well as the teachers who took responsibility for ensuring that questionnaires were administered and returned. And second, I am much indebted to members of the BMRB Class of 2002's graduate training scheme who worked with me to develop the questionnaire for the adult survey, personally undertook many of the interviews, and prepared a first analysis of the data and an initial presentation of the findings.

Many colleagues at NCB contributed in some way or another to the project. I particularly thank Jessica Datta, Emma Georgiou, Alison Love, Helen Mackenzie, Lisa Payne, Esther Poyer, Ruth Sinclair, and Jane Withey.

Outside the office, my thanks go to Berry Mayall who read through the manuscript at an early stage and offered valuable comments. The friendly and helpful support of Julia Mortimer and the team at Policy Press is also much appreciated. Last but not least, I owe much to Kevin Stenson for his encouragement during the final stages of the project.

ONE

Perceptions of childhood

While children's[1] lives have many things in common, growing up is a very individual experience. The time in question, a child's age, gender, family, culture, neighbourhood and ethnicity are but some of the factors that will determine its reality. Childhood is, in this sense, a social construction.

How is childhood seen these days? What follows is an exploration of contemporary perceptions of 'ordinary' children and adults. The purpose is to contribute to an up-to-date picture of how children, young people and adults interpret childhood and adult–child relationships. The evidence is based on a survey of 2,000 pupils at school and interviews with 500 adults, drawing on the available literature as well as current policy and practice perspectives. The setting for the research is contemporary England, the home of participating children and adults and the main source of the reported literature.

A series of everyday themes are addressed: the meaning of childhood today; growing up and becoming responsible; peer influences and parental controls; the degree to which young people are over-protected; and the quality of communication between young people and adults. Also, to what extent is England a child-friendly society? And how can children's (and adults') lives be improved? The final chapter discusses the findings and key messages arising from the research and sets them in a broader societal context. It outlines some of the attitudes and actions to be challenged and developed in the 21st century with the welfare and well-being of all children and young people in mind.

This chapter sets the scene for later discussion by considering the construction of childhood and its prevailing models. It then addresses the differences between childhood and adulthood, and asks whether the boundaries are changing. Lastly, it looks at some of the common images of childhood.

Constructing childhood

Recent decades have seen massive shifts in the status and meaning of childhood (Hendrick, 1997; Prout, 2005). While children have previously been presumed to grow up in rather uniform ways, they are now seen as actively affecting their own patterns of development and social life. Their contributions through discussion and work, their negotiations, and their struggles for power mean they can make a real difference to the course of their own lives. Children are not regarded as apprentice adults but as a social group in their own right. While they will not be children forever, their status in childhood does not rest on the fact that they will one day become adults.

An important consequence of this changed perception is the realisation that childhood cannot be understood simply through the eyes and words of adults. Children are social actors with their own voices, and they are able to speak on their own behalf. They have rights just like adults, and there is now a far greater willingness to heed, and act on, what they say.

The notion of the child as a social actor springs from the social constructionist perspective, which states that childhood is not about objective truths but understanding based on cultural setting (Stainton Rogers and Stainton Rogers, 1992). This emergent paradigm, as described by James and Prout (1997), puts the interests of the child at the fore. Along with Jenks (1996), these authors point to the limitations of accounts that posit socialisation or psychological processes as central to the child becoming an adult. These suggest largely invariant outcomes and ignore the child's individual role in the process. Although the biological immaturity of children is a fact of life, the ways in which this is understood and made meaningful is dependent on culture.

According to James and Prout (1997):

> ... childhood and children's social relationships and cultures are worthy of study in their own right, and not just in respect to the social construction by adults. This means that children must be seen as actively involved in the construction of their own social lives, the lives of those around them and of the societies in which they live. They can no longer be regarded as simply the passive subjects of structural determinations.

Other authors have expanded on these ideas. Mayall (2002) went on to discuss and demonstrate how childhood is a social category and how, in many ways, the study of childhood runs parallel to the study of women as a minority social group. Children are participants in structuring the social order, and this becomes apparent when their voices are heard. She says:

Most noticeably, young people give the lie to theories of childhood incompetence and of childhood merely as preparation; young people clearly indicate their moral engagement with issues in relationships both within and across the generations; they put high value on rights, and especially their participation rights, and on interdependence in relationships.

While childhood is viewed as a permanent component of the social structure, it is constructed in different ways at different times. This means the ways in which children contribute to the social order change. For example, and as Qvortrup (1991) has pointed out, children's social usefulness has, over recent years, shown a shift from undertaking paid work to engaging in education and learning and contributing to knowledge and a skilled labour force.

The concept of generation is thus key. It is a dimension of social organisation as important as class, gender and ethnicity in understanding children and childhood (Mayall, 2001). Members of different generations grow up with different histories and cultures, and relationships across generations have to take distinctive experiences and perspectives into account. This was illustrated by the accounts of childhood provided by three generations of women (born between 1911 and 1921, 1940 and 1948, and 1965 and 1975 respectively) from 12 kinship groups (Brannen, 2004). Stories, vocabularies and issues of significance differed according to generation even if there were also some similarities.

As generational values depend on history and culture, the divide between generations varies according to the degree and nature of social change occurring in the periods between the times adults and children grow up. Hart (2005) compares, for instance, the marked divide between the values of children and their parents in the late 1950s, particularly in relation to sex and marriage, and the much greater consensus found from the 21st *British social attitudes* survey (Phillips, 2005). It seems that differences between the generations are becoming less marked and that there is more tolerance at all ages towards sex, gender roles and family life. Some differences of opinion remain, of course, such as on lone parenthood and under-age sex, but on the whole social attitudes do not currently display such an enormous generation gap as in the past.

All these arguments and demonstrations reinforce the point that there is no single concept of childhood. All children are individuals and each is affected by a unique range of circumstances and situations, historical, social, cultural and temporal. As Lee (2001) writes:

> Growing up is as diverse in its major and minor currents, its eddies and whirlpools as is the range of human extension.

This underlines the need for many concepts of childhood. Jenks (1996) has asked:

> What do we bring to mind when we contemplate the child? Whether to regard children as pure, bestial, innocent, corrupt, charged with potential, tabula rasa, or even as we view our adult selves; whether they think and reason as we do, are immersed in a receding tide of inadequacy or are the possessors of a clarity of vision which we have through experience lost; whether their forms of language, games and conventions are alternatives to our own, imitations or crude precursors of our own now outgrown, or simply transitory impenetrable trivia which are amusing to witness and recollect; whether they are constrained and we have achieved freedom, or we have assumed constraint and they are truly free – all these considerations, and more, continue to exercise our theorizing about the child in social life.

Social perspective also makes a difference. In a later report, Jenks (2001) elaborates how

> Childhood is conceived from different social, political and moral positions, many of which are utterly reductionist and the majority are certainly unreflexive in recovering their auspices. What, if anything, might the love and anxiety of a parent, the analytical demands of a sociologist and the journalist's desire to find a story with a high moral ground have in common?

He compiles an inventory of models that includes the evil child, the innocent child, the immanent child, the naturally developing child, and the socially constructed child. Whereas the first two of these constructions reflect relatively enduring characteristics, the other three are more dependent on external forces. The immanent child, for example, is akin to the notion of an 'unfinished' human in that the child has yet to grow, develop morally and learn. This again is the idea of the child 'becoming' rather than 'being'. How that child becomes, however, depends on the experiences to which he or she is exposed. The naturally developing child, of which Rousseau's *Émile* (1762) is a good example, depends much more on the freedom and guidance to explore and learn for oneself. According to Locke's view, and the notion that individual differences are largely attributable to education, the socially constructed child depends on early training (of mental processes and perceptions) to counter lack of natural reason.

These philosophical positions highlight the complexity surrounding concepts of childhood. Reeves (2003) points out how, despite the growing child-centred political consensus:

> ... treacly words mask a deep-seated uncertainty about the nature of children and childhood. Are children mini-adults, able to manage a sophisticated consumer environment and influence events? Or are they large toddlers requiring constant protection, not least from the state, against a predatory society? Does their youthful vigour represent the long-term solution to our problems, or are their delinquency and disenchantment the cause? Perhaps most important – with whom does responsibility for their welfare rest?

> Listen to Gordon Brown, and children are the little angels who will bear us to a fairer world. Listen to Charles Clarke and they are the army of the new economy. Listen to David Blunkett and they are the thugs blighting our cities. Listen to Tony Blair and, depending on the day, they are all of the above.

The distinction between the 'good' and the 'bad' is sometimes revealed through the co-existence of these extremes. Fionda (2001) discusses this dichotomy and cites the reporting of the James Bulger murder where the innocent, dependent child is portrayed as the victim of the 'bad' and 'evil' Venables and Thompson. She also points to similar dichotomies in other spheres, such as literature, and contrasts Harry Potter and the Famous Five. She suggests that:

> In contrast with the media stereotype, the 'good' child in literature is often the one with adult-like qualities of competence, maturity and social awareness. They are often depicted fighting forces of evil (either in other 'bad' children or in adults) using cunning and ingenuity.

In addition, Fionda shows how the same person can be presented in different ways by the media. The young prostitute, for instance, may have been a victim of exploitation and abuse, yet been failed by numerous welfare workers. And offenders may also have been the victims of crime.

The role of government and the state is, moreover, stronger than mere rhetoric. Hendrick (2003) examined ways in which the meaning of childhood has been influenced by the state in recent years. He describes how, in the immediate post-war period, the welfare state was born, and optimism and liberalism prevailed. The state placed greater emphasis on preventive care and protecting children from disadvantage and adversity. Recommendations and legislation, such as the Curtis Report of 1946, the 1948 Children Act, and the Children and Young Persons Acts of 1963 and 1969, provided testimony to the changing direction. With the Conservatives and Margaret Thatcher in power from 1979, however, came different kinds of change. The later rule of New Labour meant things were on the move again. Although young people are now seen much more as contributing to the functioning of the social order, and are being prepared for citizenship, they are still held accountable for their actions and their misdemeanours are not greatly tolerated.

In other ways, too, social structure affects the meaning of childhood. Put at its most general, Qvortrup (1994) explains that it is important to indicate how:

> ... the common and general condition of children cannot be explained by reference to merely the level of the family or any other micro-level; it must in addition be understood in terms of the development of societal macro-parameters, which otherwise are availed of only in connection with adults' life conditions. It is in particular when parameters of that order interact or act against each other that childhood may be forgotten or sacrificed. No one is claiming that children's interests are deliberately undermined; on the contrary, one difficulty in the analysis of childhood is, on the one hand, the outspoken concern for children, and on the other a structural 'inconsiderateness' or 'indifference' on the side of society.

Children have very different lives depending on their social and parental background. Poverty, for example, makes a marked difference to how children are brought up and the opportunities open to them (Bradshaw,

2002). A recent report from the Institute of Public Policy Research (2004) indicates that at the time of writing around 23% of British children were living in homes earning below 60% of median income. The report also highlights how social class and ethnic background continue to influence life chances. Where children live, which often reflects these other social factors, is also significant in determining opportunities of many kinds such as in education and employment.

With such a range of factors influencing childhoods it is little wonder that, in itself, the concept of childhood can seem rather general and remote. It is also not surprising that people can hold one view of children in general and quite another of children they know. So it is understandable that one's own children can be regarded rather differently from everybody else's. In this context Aynsley-Green (2003) points to the

> ... paradox over how we personally feel about our children, and what, until very recently, society as a whole and governments in general have not felt about children.

Distinctions between childhood and adulthood

There has always been unease over the extent to which childhood and adulthood are similar or different. If similar, asks Lee (2001), should there be both a UN Declaration of Human Rights and a UN Convention on the Rights of the Child? If different, where are the boundaries between childhood and adulthood and have they become more or less distinct in recent years?

The historian Aries (1962) was among the first to suggest that childhood might be a contrived rather than a natural concept. His central thesis is that:

> ... while the traditional child was happy because he was free to mix with many classes and ages, a special condition known as childhood was 'invented' in the early modern period, resulting in a tyrannical concept of the family which destroyed friendship and sociability and deprived children of freedom, inflicting upon them for the first time the birch and the prison cell.

He describes how:

> In mediaeval society the idea of childhood did not exist;
> this is not to suggest that children were neglected, forsaken
> or despised. The idea of childhood is not to be confused
> with affection for children: it corresponds to an awareness
> of the particular nature of childhood, that particular nature
> which distinguishes the child from the adult.... In mediaeval
> society, this awareness was lacking ... as soon as the child
> could live without the constant solicitude of his mother,
> his nanny or his cradle-rocker, he belonged to adult society.

Part of Aries' argument rests on the observation that, before the Middle Ages, children were generally portrayed as miniature versions of grown-ups and given similar things to do and wear. He suggests it was a revelation when artists realised that children were not just small adults and had, for example, proportionately much larger heads than adults.

Not all writers agree with this view. Orme (2001), for instance, joins those who say that Aries' thesis, that childhood was unrecognised as a distinct period until the 16th or 17th century, is not supported by the evidence. He refers to Shakespeare's seven ages of man, and to records of children's play, to illustrated manuscripts, paintings, toys, games and books from the Middle Ages. And de Mause (1976) challenges the belief that mediaeval artists could not paint realistic children, criticising as 'fuzzy' the idea that childhood was invented.

Part of the difficulty of establishing what it has meant to be a child over the centuries is that much of what has been written is based on limited and probably biased information. According to Bossard (1948; quoted by de Mause, 1976):

> Unfortunately, the history of childhood has never been
> written, and there is some doubt whether it ever can be
> written [because] of the dearth of historical data bearing
> on childhood.

He is not alone in thinking this. De Mause (1976) himself cautions against believing everything that historians have written because "most of these works so badly distort the facts of childhood in the periods they cover". He relates how biographers often idealise childhood and write very little about its earliest years; how social historians are prone to imputing motives for actions and providing excuses even for those who have abused their children. He claims that where no happy memories can be unearthed, arguments are sometimes put forward to imply that good parents leave fewer traces than bad ones.

Historical accounts always involve selective judgement in dealing with contradictory images. Gittins (1998) observes that children were represented by Wordsworth and Blake with enthusiastic delight, while for Dickens they were more likely to be oppressed or sickly. From a social constructionist viewpoint, these differences say as much about the writers and their social or political viewpoints as about how children actually lived.

To return to the present, if we accept that childhood does exist, where are its actual boundaries? Certainly they are far from clear and consistent. Exhortations to 'grow up' and 'stay young' in almost the same breath, and an uneasy blend of permissiveness and restriction, attest to the confusion that exists. Postman (1982) has provoked discussion by suggesting that childhood itself is disappearing. His thesis is that there is a clear distinction between biological and social childhood:

> Children are the living messages we send to a time we will not see. From a biological point of view it is inconceivable that any culture will forget that it needs to reproduce itself. But it is quite possible for a culture to exist without a social idea of children. Unlike infancy, childhood is a social artefact, not a biological category. Our genes contain no clear instructions about who is and is not a child and the laws of survival do not require that a distinction be made between the world of an adult and the world of a child.

Postman (1982) voiced concern that these boundaries are becoming increasingly blurred as children and young people become more and more exposed to adult culture through new media and access to drugs, sex and other influences. Lee (2001) cites these changes to challenge the distinction between adult 'human beings' and child 'human becomings'. According to this distinction, adulthood represents the end of a journey while childhood describes the journey itself. Lee argues that as adulthood has become a less stable and predictable state (in employment and family life), childhood can no longer be defined in relation to it. In addition, the 'adult being' and 'child becoming' distinction was, to a large extent, based on adults' ability to control children's access to information. Television, computers and video have had an enormous impact. All in all, the distinction between childhood and adulthood is becoming increasingly ambiguous.

Another view is that boundaries between childhood and adulthood are becoming sharper. Mayall (2002) summarises the position and explains how children's and adults' lives are diverging. Children are increasingly protected from work, they have achieved a state of 'precious but burdensome', they are a highly protected group (from dangers of all kinds), but they are excluded from many public places (often because they are viewed as a threat, and because of traffic and 'stranger danger').

As Buckingham (2000) suggests, patterns of change are in reality complex and ambiguous:

> Contemporary changes in childhood pull in different directions at the same time. Thus, in some respects, children are becoming 'empowered', while in others they are becoming more institutionalised and subject to adult control: in some areas, the boundaries between adults and children are blurring, but in others they are being powerfully reinforced. Furthermore, I have argued that these developments affect different groups of children in different ways. Thus, childhood is indeed becoming commercialised, but there are also growing inequalities in material and cultural capital that make it difficult to talk about 'childhood' in such generalized terms.

It may also be the case that while young people grow up in some ways, they remain dependent in others. Indeed dependence may continue into early adulthood as witnessed by the increasing number of 'grown-up' young people who remain within the parental home (see below). It seems, according to Langford et al (2001), that successive governments have contributed to this increasing dependence of young people on their parents. The age at which young people qualify for Social Security, Housing Benefits and the full National Minimum Wage has increased (see Jones and Bell, 2000), and grants for higher education have, in recent years, been replaced by loans. Parents are also more responsible for their children's actions, such as in relation to education and homework (Home Office, 1998). Parenting Orders under the 1998 Crime and Disorder Act further mean that parents of young people under 16 who commit a crime may now be required to attend counselling and guidance sessions. In the view of Spender and John (2001):

> The threshold of adulthood has become steadily more diffuse through the 20th century because of the prolongation of education for many, resulting in

postponement of work choices and the need for continued financial dependence.

The main conclusion seems to be that childhood continues to exist, but that its meaning is subject to a continual process of evolution and change.

Images of childhood

Even at any point in time, however, images of children and teenagers are inconsistent and incompatible. These images are everywhere. As well as featuring as central characters in books, television and film, young people appear in advertising campaigns and fundraising initiatives. They receive enormous attention if they are victims or perpetrators of any accident, crime or abuse. These images reflect the many contemporary concepts of childhood and often capitalise on them. They are rarely neutral.

Holland (1992) examines public images of childhood and the meanings they construct. She makes a convincing case concerning the manipulation of such imagery and talks about "the wide eyes of the appealing child, the crouched body of the abused child, the structured placing of the child within the family". In her view:

> The imagery always draws on and nourishes the fantasy world of our longings. It mediates between our memory and our dreams. The nostalgia of imagery is part of the nostalgia each of us feels for a lost moment of satisfaction and a longing for a future of reconciliation and peace. This is a theme to which the imagery of childhood is well suited.

She adds how:

> The multiple narratives of childhood built up by the imagery are far from consistent as they move between the different contexts of commerce, information and welfare. But as they play the image, recurring themes can be identified, echoing back and forth between them. The familiar typology of childhood includes the energetic boy and the seductive girl, the dependent child in need of protection, the ignorant child in need of education, the playful child in the home and the violent child on the streets. Sometimes pictures of children differentiate sharply

between girls and boys; at other times the signifiers of age dominate those of gender. Some images are well developed, with many variations, but others appear less frequently and fit uneasily into the patterns of public presentation.

A young person's age plays an important role in portrayal. With their appealing rounded features, babies are often used to convey contentment and symbolise motherhood and family life. Infants may be presented in a similar way, but once the soft features disappear and the 'gangly youth' appears, it can be a different story. Harry Enfield's television character Kevin is an exaggerated portrait of a teenager yet one that is recognisable to many parents.

As images reflect contemporary meanings of childhood, culture is also important. Gram (2004) examined 290 advertisements for children's products published in French, Dutch and German women's magazines between 1995 and 1998. While inevitably there were similarities, there were also differences in the way that play, intellectual development, and well-being were presented.

This contrast in the representation of children and teenagers was remarked on by Holland (1992):

> The public imagery of childhood tends to take itself for granted. It rarely reflects or comments on its own construction. Not so with the imagery of youth. 'Youth' has regularly made the front pages of the popular press....
> It makes up both the readership and the topic of magazines on style, fashion and music. The characteristics of youth have been endlessly nagged over and studied. Images of youth have been examined and dissected, catalogued and discussed, as if the image itself could give some clue to the nature of this elusive phenomenon ... the indications of childhood are no longer appropriate, and those of adulthood are withheld or refused....

All manner of images of youth have been presented, but perhaps the negative have predominated. While some, such as Harry Enfield's Kevin, exist mainly for amusement, there is a danger that some of the less positive images may reflect society's preoccupations as well as help mould them. Kidd-Hewitt and Osborne (1995) ask whether media reporting of crime, by unfairly stereotyping certain individuals and groups, instils 'moral panic' and a general fear of crime in the population at large. Certainly the media are frequently blamed for whipping up public hysteria. Smith (2003) discusses perceptions of criminal behaviour and how they are intensified by the media (as well as political interests and the judiciary). The outcome, he suggests, is a heightened public sensitivity to certain offences such as street crime, and greater readiness to deal harshly with such behaviour.

Recent criticism of the media has often focused on the portrayal of violent adolescents on the front pages of both tabloids and broadsheets. The imagery can be shocking and inevitably has an impact. Headlines referring to young people as 'Hell cat, age 11', 'Untouchable yob, aged 11', 'Hell's children', 'Bad boys' and 'Teen thugs' are illustrative of this. Whether or not these images of violent children are in any sense justified, they undoubtedly give the impression that such behaviour is more common than is the case. They are also likely to increase people's fear of young people, and of being out alone, especially at night. A recent survey of press articles in the main national daily newspapers and a selection of big regional titles, carried out by MORI (2004) over the period of one week, confirmed how one in three youth-related articles were about crime. Furthermore, the vast majority were negative in tone, with only 14% depicting a purely positive image and 15% adopting a neutral tone.

Other recent and memorable images of children are presented for different purposes. The shocking picture of the 'baby bomber', an image of a Palestinian baby dressed as a suicide bomber said to be a family photograph taken as a joke, was shown worldwide in newspapers and on television screens and caused an outrage. By contrast, the picture of goalkeeper David Seaman holding his angelic looking daughter was no doubt used to soften the blow as he returned home, blaming himself, after England lost to Brazil in the quarter-finals of the World Cup. Graphic photographs of young boys seen building barriers on a railway track were part of yet another agenda about how some children occupy themselves during the school holidays.

Childhood has always have been depicted in art and literary fiction. Zipes (2001) charts the moral and cultural values in children's literature over recent generations. He wonders about the influence of widely-read popular books, such as the Harry Potter series. On the homogenisation of children he writes:

> Making children all alike is, sadly, a phenomenon of our times.... I have always written with the hope that childhood might be redeemed, not innocent childhood, but a childhood rich in adventure and opportunities for self-exploration and self-determination. Instead, I witness a

growing regulation and standardisation of children's lives that undermine the very sincere concern parents have for their young. It appears that my hope for greater freedom and creativity in children's lives will be disappointed.

The imagery of childhood provides a social narrative (Holland, 2004). Ultimately, perhaps, one purpose is to challenge the status quo and make people think. Some images of young people present their own contradictory messages. We see pregnant schoolgirls, child parents, same-sex parents, and children born to elderly or widowed mothers. The full diversity of childhood is on view. The language is often as important as the imagery. "What's the difference between a wild child and a yob?" asks Curtis (2002). "None, except that the wild child has rich parents," he retorts.

The rest of the book

The survey methodology used to gain the views of some 2,000 children and young people and 500 adults on the meaning and reality of contemporary childhood is described in the next chapter. The following seven chapters then outline current issues of childhood: the experience of being a child; growing up and becoming an 'adult'; the influences, controls and protection that impinge on young lives; status and respect; relationships between child and adult generations; the characteristics of a child-friendly society; and children's and adults' concerns and priorities for action and change. The final chapter draws together the key findings and messages and suggests how developments in policy and practice might signal improvements in well-being and welfare for children today.

Note
[1] The terms 'children' and 'young people' are used interchangeably throughout this book. Where appropriate, any distinctions by age are made explicit, for example, by distinguishing between primary school and secondary school level children.

TWO

Collecting the evidence

Two new surveys were carried out for this report to provide up-to-date information on young people's and adults' attitudes to growing up in England. These two surveys are referred to as the school survey and the adult survey.

The school survey

The main purpose of the school survey was to collect views from children and teenagers of all ages on what it is like to be a child in England, and how older and younger generations seem to get on together. To compare what young people and adults say on these matters, many questions were similar to those included in the adult survey.

The questionnaire

Two versions of a short self-completion questionnaire were developed, for children at primary schools and at secondary schools. The questions in the two schedules were very similar, but some were phrased differently to make them more suitable for the age group in question. The only question that older, but not younger, children were asked was the age at which young people should take responsibility and achieve independence in various areas (see below). These questions did not seem appropriate for children as young as 7 to 8 years in Year 3.

The main areas covered in the questionnaire for children were:

- Background information (gender, ethnicity, school year, and household members).
- Whether or not England is child-friendly (are adults friendly to young people of their age? do they feel welcome in places like shops, restaurants and leisure centres? what would they do for young people of their age if they were Prime Minister? do they think England is a good country to

grow up in? do adults enjoy seeing children playing in their neighbourhood?).

- Doing things with adults (do parents and other adults usually enjoy spending time with children and young people of their age? do children and young people of their age usually enjoy spending time with parents and other adults?).

- Being polite and showing respect (primary school level children were asked whether children of their age are polite enough to adults and whether adults are polite enough to them; secondary school level children were asked a similar question but in relation to respect rather than politeness).

- Talking and listening (do parents spend enough time talking to children and young people of their age, and do children and young people of their age spend enough time talking to their parents? do adults listen to children and young people properly, and do children and young people listen to adults properly? do parents and carers take notice of what they think and want [primary level] or do adults care about what young people think and want [secondary level]?).

- Growing up (do children and young people grow up too quickly these days? do children and young people of their age have to make too many decisions for themselves? do parents and carers let them choose their own clothes and hairstyles [primary level] or are adults tolerant of young people's clothes and hairstyles [secondary level]? do parents and carers worry too much about them hurting themselves or being in danger [primary level] or do parents over-protect their children [secondary level]?).

- Influences on children and young people (which of the following have the strongest influence on young people and their ideas: parents, brothers and sisters, friends, media, teachers, and other?).

- At what age? (secondary level only) (when should young people be held legally responsible for their actions if they commit a crime such as shoplifting, graffiti or street crime? when should they start to learn about sex and relationships at school? when should they be able to visit their doctor on their own without a parent or other adult? when should a young person be able to baby-sit for someone else's children?).

- Their childhood (are children and young people mostly happy? are their childhoods strict? how often do their parents and carers really listen to them and take their views into account? do they have enough things to do in their leisure time out of school?).

- Best and worst things (what in their own words are the best and worst things about being a child or young person of their age).

• Making lives happier and more enjoyable (primary school children were asked to suggest two things adults could do to make children happier and two things children could do to make adults happier, and those at secondary level were asked to suggest two things adults could do to make life easier and more enjoyable for children and young people in England as well as two things children and young people could do to make life easier and more enjoyable for adults).

The sample

Twelve schools were approached and asked if they would take part in the survey, and 11 of these agreed to participate. These schools were selected from northern and southern parts of England and from city areas as well as more rural settings. They were in the main schools that the author had had prior contact with for other research purposes. They are likely to have been fairly representative of schools nationally, but school data was not collected to be able to demonstrate this. In selecting them, however, the author did ensure that they included a good span of schools of different sizes and in different locations.

Of the 11 participating schools, five were primary and six were secondary level. As the secondary schools tended to be larger than the primary schools, there were more older than younger children in the sample overall. Schools were asked to include as many children as possible in the survey, and the numbers that took part at each school are shown below (Table 2.1).

Between 16 and 176 children participated at each of the five primary schools and between 48 and 447 at the six secondary schools.

Table 2.1: The school survey sample by school and gender

School	Number of children in the survey			
	Males	Females	NK	Total
Primary 1	31	48	1	80
Primary 2	47	42	–	89
Primary 3	96	77	3	176
Primary 4	10	6	–	16
Primary 5	12	12	–	24
Secondary 6	213	173	4	390
Secondary 7	–	427	–	427
Secondary 8	24	24	–	48
Secondary 9	60	–	–	60
Secondary 10	211	229	7	447
Secondary 11	138	142	5	285
Total	842	1,180	20	2,042

Questionnaires were administered by class teachers. These were sent to schools with instructions on how they should be introduced and completed. It was indicated that the schedules should take no longer than 20 minutes to complete, that pupils should not compare notes or discuss questions, that some assistance could be offered if a child had particular difficulty understanding a question, and that all questionnaires should be collected at the end of the session. Teachers were asked to reinforce that there was no need to put names on the questionnaires and that all information would be regarded as strictly confidential by the research team.

A total of 385 primary and 1,657 secondary school children took part in the survey and completed questionnaires. Those at primary level were fairly evenly divided by gender, but there were more girls than boys at secondary level: although there was one all girls and one all boys secondary school, many more children from the former took part in the survey. For purposes of analysis, the full sample was subdivided by age into four sub-groups, two at primary and two at secondary level. The younger primary group included those from Years 3 to 5 (7 to 10-year-olds), and the older primary group comprised those from Years 6 and 7 (10 to 12-year-olds). At secondary level, the younger group included those in Years 7 and 8 (11 to 13-year-olds) and the older group any children above this age. The characteristics of the full sample by gender and age group are shown below (Table 2.2).

Children were asked how they would describe themselves, and given the options of White, Black-Caribbean, Black-African, Indian, Pakistani, Bangladeshi, Chinese, Mixed, or 'Something else' (which they were asked to describe). Most answered this question, and Figure 2.1 shows the pattern of responses for the valid sample as a whole.

Overall, seven in ten children described themselves as White and roughly similar proportions (about one in 20 or 25) described themselves as Black-Caribbean, Black- African, Indian, Mixed, and 'Something else'. Smaller numbers said they were Pakistani, Bangladeshi or Chinese. For purposes of analysis, children were reclassified into

Table 2.2: The school survey sample by age group and gender

	Males	Females	Total
Younger primary (years 3,4,5)	111	100	211
Older primary (years 6,7)	84	84	168
Younger secondary (years 7,8)	318	491	806
Older secondary (years 9+)	322	497	816
Total	835	1,172	2,027*

*The total does not tally with the total in Table 2.1 as some children did not indicate their school year and some of these also gave no indication of their gender.

Figure 2.1: Children in the school survey by ethnicity (*n*=2,023)

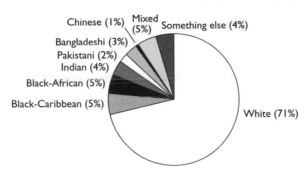

two categories, 'White' and 'Other ethnicity'. It is fully acknowledged that this 'Other ethnicity' group is highly heterogeneous, and that any effects attributable to ethnicity can only be speculative. Nonetheless, the small numbers in the other groups make reclassification necessary.

On the basis of this reclassification, marked differences between schools emerged with the proportions calling themselves 'White' ranging from 30% to 94% in primary schools, and from 8% to 99% in secondary schools. Not unexpectedly, the schools with high proportions of 'Other ethnicity' children were found in inner-city areas while those with low proportions were in other types of location across the country.

There were both gender and age patterns within this reclassified sample. First, more girls than boys fell within the 'Other ethnicity' group, as shown below (Figure 2.2).

Figure 2.2: The school survey sample by ethnicity and gender

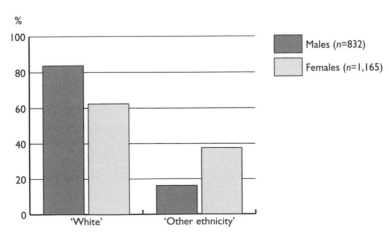

Figure 2.3: The school survey sample by ethnicity and age

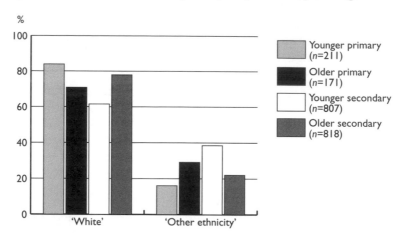

And second, there was some variation in ethnicity across the four age groupings (Figure 2.3).

As a further background question, children were asked who lived at home with them at the moment. This was an open-ended question, but responses were coded according to whether they mentioned two parents, one parent only, or some other arrangement including time spent with both parents. It was also noted whether or not they said they had siblings at home. Overall, about three quarters lived with two parents and most of the rest lived with one parent, usually their mother. Well over four in five mentioned brothers and sisters.

Analysis and presentation of the data

All survey data were coded and analysed using SPSS software. Chi-square statistical tests were applied, as appropriate, to identify particularly strong patterns and trends. Differences between sub-groups of children were examined by age, gender and ethnicity. Responses to open-ended questions were transcribed and recoded into dominant categories, as outlined in subsequent chapters.

The adult survey

An adult survey was carried out to complement the pupil survey and provide greater understanding of adults' attitudes towards children and young people in contemporary England. Specifically, it aimed to:

- investigate adults' opinions on the problems and issues faced and created by young people;
- identify characteristics of a child-friendly society and determine how far England is thought of as child friendly;
- explore the differences between adults who have contact with children and those who do not;
- discover different views based on age, gender, parenthood, contact with children and social grade;
- assess the role of the media.

The interviews

The adult survey was undertaken in collaboration with the British Market Research Bureau (BMRB). Using a questionnaire developed jointly by the author and the BMRB Class of 2002's graduate training scheme, a total of 507 completed interviews were carried out with adults, defined as those aged 20 years and above, in their own homes using Computer-assisted Personal Interviewing (CAPI) techniques. Each interview lasted between 20 and 25 minutes and all took place during July 2002. A total of 152 home visits were carried out by members of the Class of 2002 and the rest (362) were undertaken by members of the BMRB face-to-face interviewing panel. All interviewers, including members of the Class of 2002, were fully trained in accordance with Market Research Society (MRS) standards. BMRB is a member of the Interviewer Quality Control Scheme as well as the MRS Interviewer Identity Card Scheme.

The interview sample was selected to be nationally representative of adults in terms of age, gender, social grade and region of residence. Parents as well as non-parents were included to enable comparisons to be made between these two groups. BMRB's Random Locale sampling method was used. This drew respondents from a small set of homogeneous streets selected with probability proportional to population after stratification by their ACORN characteristics and region. ACORN (A Classification of Residential Neighbourhoods) is a system based on Census measures allowing localised residential areas to be classified according to the types of people mainly living in them. By pre-selecting areas in which to interview based on their ACORN type, a representative spread of social grades in England could be ensured. Some consideration was also paid to enlisting respondents within the proximity of an available interviewer.

The sample

Of the adults who took part in the survey, 42% were men and 59% women. This no doubt reflected the greater likelihood that women were at home at the times when the interviewers visited. The age distribution of this sample is shown below. Participants ranged from around 20 years to over 65 years, and there were higher proportions of participants in the younger than older age groups.

Figure 2.4: The adult survey sample by age

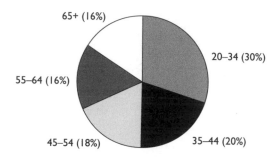

Information on social grade was also collected, largely to confirm that a representative sample had been achieved. On the basis of responses to a series of pre-established questions, participants were assigned to one of four categories: AB, C1, C2, and DE (Table 2.3). The distribution of participants according to this rating is shown below (Figure 2.5). The highest proportion fell within the C1 classification, and the smallest proportion within the AB grouping.

Figure 2.5: The adult survey sample by social grade

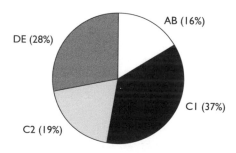

Table 2.3: Social grades classification

Grade	Social status	Occupation of chief income earner
A	Upper middle class	Higher managerial administrative or professional occupations. Top level civil servants.
		Retired people previously graded A with a pension from their job and widows/widowers if they are receiving a pension from their late spouse's job.
B	Middle class	Intermediate managerial administrative or professional people. Senior officers in local government and civil service.
		Retired people previously graded B with a pension from their job and widows/widowers if they are receiving a pension from their late spouse's job.
C1	Lower middle class	Supervisory or clerical and junior managerial administrative or professional occupations.
		Retired people previously graded C1 with a pension from their job and widows/widowers if they are receiving a pension from their late spouse's job.
C2	Skilled working class	Skilled manual workers.
		Retired people previously graded C2 with a pension from their job and widows/widowers if they are receiving a pension from their late spouse's job.
D	Working class	Semi and unskilled manual workers.
		Retired people previously graded D with a pension from their job and widows/widowers if they are receiving a pension from their late spouse's job.
E	Those at lowest levels of subsistence	All those entirely dependent on the State long term through sickness unemployment old age or other reasons.
		Casual workers and those without a regular income.

Analysis and presentation of the data

Although Random Locale is an effective way of accessing a high quality representative sample, face-to-face interviewing does tend inherently to over- and under-represent certain groups of people. Five age bands (20-34, 35-44, 45-54, 55-64, 65+) were selected and quotas were accordingly set on the lower and upper age bands of the adult population interviewed. A minimum quota of 100 interviews was set for those aged 20-34 and a maximum quota of 100 interviews with those aged 65 years or more. Numbers in the middle age groups fell out naturally giving around 100 interviews in each age band. Non-interlocking quotas were also set on gender so that approximately half the total number of interviews would be carried out with men and half with women. This is broadly representative of gender within the English population of adults aged 20 years and above which comprises approximately 49% men and 51% women.

In addition to these approaches to sampling, the resultant data were weighted in order to make them as nationally representative as possible. The following table (Table 2.4) indicates the adjustments that were made.

Survey data were transferred into an SPSS datafile and analysed in a similar way to the information from the school survey. Response patterns were examined by age, gender, social grade, parenthood and contact with children.

Verbatim quotations from adults are presented throughout this book. Some of these were collected at focus groups carried out to inform the development of the questionnaire and others were gathered during the course of the main survey. Additional details on respondents (for example, age group and parent or non-parent) are available for the first of these sources only.

Table 2.4: The adult survey sample by gender, age and social grade: actual survey data and weighted percentages

	Actual survey data (%)	Weighted to England (TGI/ONS) (%)
Sex		
Men	41.6	48.7*
Women	58.4	51.3*
Age		
20-34	30.0	27.9*
35-44	20.2	20.1*
45-54	17.9	17.5*
55-64	16.1	13.7*
65+	15.8	20.8*
Social Grade		
AB	16.2	23.9**
C1	36.4	27.1**
C2	19.3	20.7**
DE	28.2	28.3**

* ONS data (population estimate at mid 2000 for England, all those aged 20+)

** TGI data (GB TGI 2002 Spring: January 2001-December 2001)

"

"Most children do too much and don't have time just to be children — too many extracurricular activities." (adult)

"Young people are fresh and quite new to the world so they are very active." (male, Year 8)

"You have your life ahead of you and you can choose what you want to be and do." (female, Year 11)

"People don't take you seriously because you are young. They think you don't know much." (female, Year 11)

"I don't like being my age because my big brother and sister always pick on me." (female, Year 5)

"Adults could realise that not all teenagers are out to do something wrong and understand that we are actually nice." (male, Year 10)

"Kids have no defined roles to live up to nowadays." (adult)

"

THREE

What's it like being a child?

What is it really like to be a child growing up in England these days? Is it a happy time? Is there too much to worry about? What are the best and worst aspects of being young? This chapter looks at how children and young people perceive their childhoods and the constraints they face. It also reports on how adults remember their own childhoods.

Happy childhoods?

All childhoods are different and, not surprisingly, the existing evidence suggests that most young people are reasonably content most of the time while some are very unhappy.

Several studies are illustrative. Ghate and Daniels (1997) found that around three quarters of a sample of almost 1,000 8- to 15-year-olds growing up in the 1990s regarded themselves as happy. All the same, over one in three, and more girls than boys, said they were 'sometimes sad' Having friends, doing things with friends, or going out with friends, followed by doing things with family members, 'getting presents' or 'having birthdays', were the things that most commonly made them happy. Taking part in or watching sports, and doing well at school, were also commonly mentioned. 'Other people being hurt, frail, sick or upset' (mentioned by a third of the sample overall but by more girls than boys), being left out, feeling excluded, or breaking up with friends, made them sad.

Children's happiness may depend, to some degree, on context. Madge and Franklin (2003) asked almost 3,000 young people at secondary school how happy they were at home and at school, and found that although there was a significant correlation between those feeling happy at home and at school, children were more likely to report feeling happy at home than at school. Overall, 89% of boys said they were always or often happy at home while 58% said they were always or often happy at school. For girls, the proportions were 84% and 66%.

Balding (2002) examined self-esteem, which seemed related to happiness, among almost 16,000 primary and secondary children. The majority of pupils showed medium or high self-esteem, but a significant minority did not. At all ages, more males had high self-esteem and more females had low self-esteem – although gender differences were not found in all schools. Overall, more than half seemed satisfied with their life at the moment, and fewer than one in five said they were not. Boys were more satisfied than girls, and girls became more dissatisfied as they grew older.

There are both happy and less happy childhoods and, as Holland (1992) points out, it is important to recognise the existence of both:

> Without the image of the unhappy child, our contemporary concept of childhood would be incomplete. Real children suffer in many different ways and for many different reasons, but pictures of sorrowing children recall those defining characteristics of childhood: dependence and powerlessness.

As an illustration of a suffering child, Gittins (1998) charts her own unhappy times and many years of therapy, and comments:

> I do not mean to neglect or ignore the more positive and happy aspects of 'the child' and 'childhood', which undoubtedly mean an enormous amount to all of us. Rather, I am interested in the contradictions between the positive ideas and hopes for 'the child', and the irrational, apparently dark and negative ways in which adults frequently act towards children, and, indeed, how children themselves can behave in ways adults regard as unacceptable and transgressive. Crucial to my argument overall is that only by trying to take on board the more negative and unacceptable aspects both of ourselves and of children are we likely to be able to move towards change.

The findings

To gain more evidence on this issue, young people in our survey were asked how happy they were. Adults were asked to contrast the lives of children nowadays and when they themselves were young.

Nine in ten children described their childhoods as very happy or quite happy rather than quite unhappy or very unhappy. There were, however, some variations by age and gender although none according to ethnicity. More younger than older children at both primary and secondary schools, for instance, said they were happy (Figure 3.1).

Figure 3.1: Happy childhoods? Responses of children by age

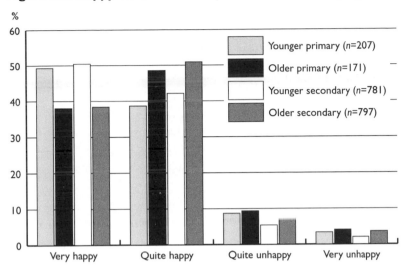

This is intriguing but difficult to explain. Girls also tended to be happier than boys, although more so at primary than secondary level.

To see how far things had changed over the past generation, adults were asked about their own childhoods and whether or not these had been happy. They seemed to say much the same as the children. Overall, 49% had been very happy and 37% had been quite happy. A further 9% seemed to have been neither happy nor unhappy and the remaining 5% reported a quite unhappy or a very unhappy childhood. Young people and adults did not paint too dissimilar pictures of their childhoods and children seemed equally likely to be happy nowadays as a generation ago.

Worries and concerns

All ages bring things to worry about and the childhood and teenage years are no exception. Looks, family and school emerged as the main concerns of more than 37,000 young people aged between 12 and 15 years and attending 122 secondary schools around the UK (Balding et al, 1998), and for girls, worrying about looks stood out above anything else. Gambling and drinking came at the bottom of the list (of the possible options), while money, health, career, unemployment, HIV/AIDS, smoking and drugs came somewhere in between. A comparison of findings with earlier years led Balding et al (1998) to conclude that worries about drugs, family, friends, and maybe also school, were becoming more common but that worrying about HIV/AIDS and gambling was on the wane. A later report on trends up to 2003 (SHEU, 2005) found some subsequent changes and in particular a downward trend in worrying about looks. It remained the main concern for about half the 14-year-old females and four in ten of the 12- to 13-year-olds, but it was most likely to be a worry for those who wanted to lose weight. Worrying about their looks had by 2003 become only the third most important concern for boys.

Whittaker et al (1998) looked at what children say about things they do and do not like about school. Friendships (63%), followed by their favourite subjects (25%), were what made the 2,527 young people taking part in the survey most happy at school. The main things that made them unhappy were: bullying (mentioned by 33%), having to study subjects they did not like (25%), unfairness (16%), and falling out with friends (14%).

Feeling unsafe in the community is another concern felt by many young people. A recent survey by MORI (2002) illustrated how similar proportions (around 42%) feel unsafe 'walking around their local area alone in the dark', as feel safe. Worries about becoming a victim of crime are high, and about half the young people in the survey said they were fearful of theft and physical assault. Over half of the 'Non-White' young people were also concerned about the possibility of racism. These fears appeared to have some basis as half the survey respondents said they had been affected by crime during the previous year and mentioned theft (24%), threatening behaviour (27%), and bullying (17%).

These studies illustrate some of the things children are concerned about. Balding et al (1998) comment how modest levels of worry are not just normal but may also have good effects in building up resilience and encouraging problem solving. It is evident, nonetheless, that high levels are a cause for concern.

The findings

So, did the young people in the surveys feel they had too much to worry about? They were asked whether there are lots of things to worry about at their age and asked to say 'yes, a lot', 'yes, quite a lot, 'no, not really', or 'don't know'. Figure 3.2 shows their mixed responses. The youngest and oldest groups were most likely to say they had lots to worry about.

Interesting differences emerged according to gender and age. Although, overall, the same proportion (23%) of males and females

Figure 3.2: Do children and young people have a lot to worry about? Responses of children by age

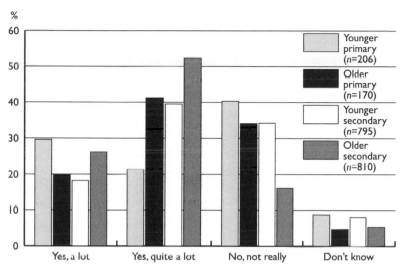

thought young people of their age had a lot to worry about, age made a difference. Among the primary groups, boys were more than one-and-a-half times as likely as girls to say they had lots to worry about. A similar, but much less marked, tendency was found for the younger secondary group. Within the older secondary group, however, girls were considerably more likely than boys to report both 'a lot' and 'quite a lot' of worries. Thus 87% of girls said that young people of their age had either a lot or quite a lot of worries while the same was true of only 66% of the males.

The best and worst things about being a child or young person

Young people were not asked directly about the things that concerned and worried them most, but they were given the opportunity to say the best and worst things about being a child or young person.

The best things

Primary school children were asked to write down one thing they liked about being a child of their age and secondary school children were asked to note one of the best things about being a young person of their age. Their many different answers were grouped according to

10 main themes. These were: things to do; computers and television; worries and responsibilities; being young; growing up; having fun; being given and bought things; family; friends; and school. A number of responses did not fit into any of these categories and were classified as 'other'.

Having few worries and responsibilities was the outstanding advantage of being young for all young people, whether male or female, and was mentioned spontaneously by almost three in ten (Figures 3.3 and 3.4). Apart from this, however, males were much more likely than females to mention things to do, computers and television, while females talked more about growing up, having fun, family and friends. Age also made a difference. In particular, children seemed to become less satisfied with their leisure activities as they got older, and computers and television seemed to play a lesser role. On the other hand, they became more likely to acknowledge their lack of worries and responsibilities as well as an ability to have fun.

For young people, few worries and responsibilities meant being young, having freedom and choice, getting their own way and doing what they liked. There was not a lot to worry about, and certainly no worries about money, going to work, paying rent or bills, thinking about problems, doing chores, taking responsibility for children, or

Figure 3.3: The best things about being a child or young person. Responses of children by gender

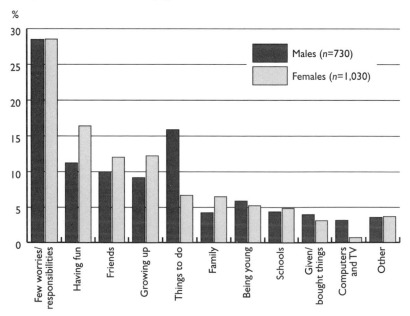

Figure 3.4: The best things about being a child or young person. Responses of children by age

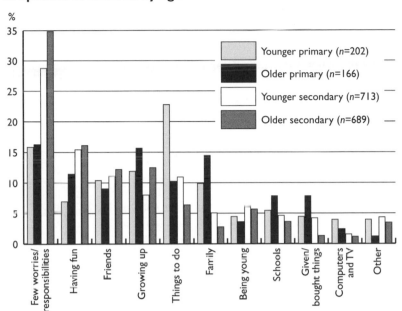

going to war. They felt that everything was done for them, they could get away with anything, and that choices and mistakes were their own.

Having fun, being happy and having lots of opportunities also meant adventures, getting excited about small things, experiencing different things, and taking part in parties, birthdays and other celebrations. "It's exciting!" was how one child described his life.

Growing up brought other advantages too. Having responsibility and being trusted more, earning money from a job, being allowed out and doing things on your own, staying up and out late, experiencing more of life, and feeling older and more grown up, were among the things children mentioned. They also said they liked having their own room, showing younger children how to behave, and gaining more respect from adults. Other benefits were being able to go shopping, wear nice clothes and be fashionable, make mistakes and learn from them, experience teenage love, and be the biggest in the school. All in all, most young people enjoyed getting older. As one said, parents have to be nice to get you to do things and, although you have more independence, you can always fall back on parents.

Having things to do meant different things for young people, and activities mentioned included skateboarding, diving, swimming, football, going to the park, climbing trees, playing on bikes, or going on holidays and trips. The main point seemed to be that they have plenty of spare time and enjoy the things that occupy them.

Families were also important to young people. Spending time with parents and siblings, being looked after and being paid attention, were among the things they valued. Some said they liked seeing their parents every day, playing with them, being listened to and helped. They talked about being loved by their parents, and one particularly liked "cuddling her nan and granddad". Having brothers and sisters and playing with them, as well as "my mum's cooking" were also mentioned.

Being young meant having one's whole life ahead, being able to start out at something and work all the way up, being fit and healthy, and looking younger and beautiful. Young people mentioned how they had enough time to decide on a career and think about the future, as well as lots of energy. Some said that they saw the world in a different way – and one added that you can beat your parents at a lot of things!

A few young people talked appreciatively about their schools and learning. Many felt they received a good and free education as well as training for a future job. One referred to "the tension of getting into a good secondary school, and then looking forward to going to a new school". Nice teachers, and not having lots of homework, were seen as other positive aspects of school.

Being given and bought things was also mentioned by some who realised how spoilt they were in getting lots of pocket money as well as other things they wanted. They pointed out how everything is free and bought for them.

The worst things

The worst things about being a child or young person generally mirrored the best things. Comments were grouped into ten categories which were: growing up; restrictions; school; being told off; not being taken seriously; having to do jobs and chores; feeling under stress; the environment; friends; and family. An 'other' category included comments that did not fall within any of these ten categories.

Three aspects stood out as disadvantages of being a child or young person. These were, in order, restrictions, school, and not being taken seriously. Gender and age again made some difference to what children said (Figures 3.5 and 3.6). Most noticeably, boys were more concerned about restrictions and school, while girls were more likely to say they disliked not being taken seriously, growing up, and elements of family

Figure 3.5: The worst things about being a child or young person. Responses of children by gender

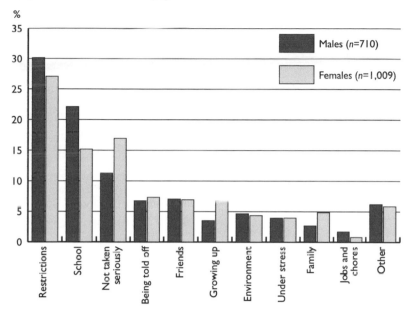

Figure 3.6: The worst things about being a child or young person. Responses of children by age

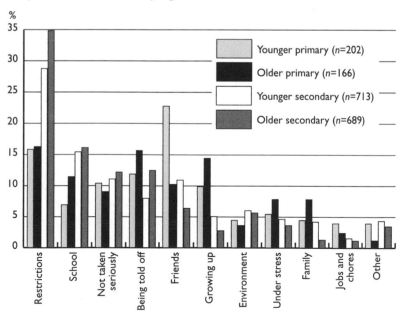

life. A dislike of restrictions and not being taken seriously were mentioned more as children got older, whereas being told off and friends were mentioned less.

Age restrictions, and a lack of freedom and independence, are what young people most disliked about their age. Not being able to see 18-rated films, go clubbing or to the pub, vote, buy lottery tickets, drive a car, look after younger children and baby-sit, drink, get a job, stay up late or stay at home on their own, were some of the things they mentioned. They felt that they could not make a lot of choices themselves, could not do what they wanted to do and get what they wanted, and that there were different rules for children and adults. In addition, they felt that they were not considered mature, did not have enough pocket money, needed permission to do things, and were always having to listen to adults.

School was also disliked. Homework, examinations, tests, Statutory Assessment Tasks (SATS), getting into trouble, detentions, and having to do sport, were some of the aspects mentioned.

A number of young people felt that they were not taken seriously by adults and were treated as 'inferior' in some way. They felt ignored, taken advantage of, misunderstood, patronised, and taken for granted. Adults often made them feel embarrassed and judged them by their clothes. Some suggested that adults do not really care about "kids".

Being told off, shouted at, and nagged are other things children did not like. Also, they resented having to do jobs and chores at home, and look after pets and younger brothers and sisters. Other problems at home included difficulties with parents and families, such as parents who worry and are over-protective, parental divorce, siblings getting them into trouble, parents not giving them enough space, being stuck in the middle when parents argue, strict parents, and not having a brother or sister. Problems with friends and peers, such as not enough friends or lacking a girlfriend or boyfriend, peer pressure, bullying and people keeping secrets, are other interpersonal difficulties they mentioned.

Other negative features were growing up, trying to grow up too quickly, puberty, getting spots, being given responsibility, the need to make decisions and be mature, getting into smoking, going to the shops alone, and paying for things themselves. What worried one boy was "Not knowing what will happen to you next – but knowing that one day I will have to leave home".

Some young people felt under stress, had problems and worries, but were unhappy and alone. Some were nervous, shy and embarrassed, and did not always think they were made welcome. Others said they had to learn the hard way, and became worried if they were not sure that other big children were around when they might be in danger. Not feeling safe, fear of violence and sexual abuse, crime and vandalism, drugs and drug dealers, kidnapping, racism and stranger danger are aspects of the wider environment that young people disliked.

Not all young people, however, could think of any disadvantages of being young. As one commented: "there is nothing I don't like about my age".

Summary

- Most children described their own lives as happy rather than unhappy. Girls, particularly at primary school level, were more likely than boys to say they had happy childhoods.
- The proportion of adults and children saying their childhoods were happy were broadly comparable.
- More than half the children said they have a lot, or quite a lot, to worry about. The oldest of the four groups of children were most likely to take this view. Within this group, the vast majority of girls, and two in three boys, thought that young people of their age have a lot or quite a lot to worry about.
- Few worries and responsibilities, nonetheless, stood out as the best thing about being a child or young person. This was true largely regardless of age and gender. Having fun, friends, growing up, things to do, and family were also important.
- The three worst aspects of being a child or young person were, in order, feeling restricted, school, and not being taken seriously.

> "Things have changed since we were young! I think the percentage of good kids and bad kids would be roughly the same now as it was when we were growing up. What has changed is what kids are allowed to see and what they would not have been allowed to see. Therefore they grow up faster." (adult)
>
> "What I like about being 11 is some adults think you have matured so you can walk around by yourself and have proper discussions." (female, Year 6)
>
> "I am at the in-between age. I am not a teenager or a grown up but I am not a little kid any more. Some people don't know how to treat me." (male, Year 6)
>
> "It seems like teenage [lifestyle] doesn't start as a numerical teenager. It starts from about eight now. I think it depends on the child. Some children are more streetwise than others…." (adult participant in focus group: 20- to 34-year-old non-parent)
>
> "Children are not given the same amount of freedom here. Kids are made to grow up too quickly." (adult participant in focus group: parent)

FOUR

Growing up, becoming an 'adult'

Central to the concept of childhood is when childhood ceases and when a child becomes an adult. Is there, or should there be, a single point of transition, or is adulthood achieved over time as maturity and increased responsibility are gained in different areas? The fundamental question seems to be whether children and adults are inherently different in some fundamental way, and passing from childhood reflects a specific stage of development, or whether adulthood is more notional and dependent on when adults, for whatever reason, think young people should become independent and responsible.

While there is some validity in Rousseau's (1762) view that childhood has "its own ways of seeing, thinking and feeling" which emerge as children grow up in their natural surroundings, it is also evident that children's development in different areas does not run parallel and that it may not be appropriate, for example, for young people to be allowed to drive a car at the same age as they are expected to take responsibility for their behaviour and actions. Of course, as James and Prout (1997) point out, vague and uncertain boundaries between childhood and adulthood make them problematic for sociological analysis.

This chapter addresses the considerable inconsistency and confusion surrounding accounts of growing up and achieving independence by asking young people and adults about transition points to young adulthood, as well as their views on questions such as whether children are growing up too quickly or whether they have to make too many decisions for themselves. First, however, the context is set by briefly outlining some of the outward signs of growing up, and examining legal restrictions on the ages at which young people are allowed to act in their own right, or required to take responsibility for their own actions.

Physical and biological maturity

The most evident and indisputable signs of growing up are the physical and biological changes that take place during puberty. These occur universally, but it is how they are understood and viewed within cultures that contributes to concepts of childhood. Growing taller is the most dramatic and visible aspect of growing physical maturity, and the pubertal growth rate doubles in speed and is greater than at any time since about two years of age. The growth spurt usually occurs in girls between about 10-and-a-half and 14 years, and in boys between around 12 and 16. Muscular growth and changes in the composition and distribution of fat occur at the same time. The lungs, heart and other bodily organs mature, and adult reproductive and sexual characteristics develop. Appearances change and young people, especially boys, become physically stronger.

Despite the fact that almost all young people pass through the same stages during puberty, there is some evidence that the whole process may now be occurring at a much younger age than in the past. The Children of the Nineties study (Peek, 2000) followed 14,000 children from birth to eight and indicated that half of all girls in Britain now enter puberty by the age of 10. In addition, one in 14 eight-year-old boys, compared with one in 150 in the previous generation, already had pubic hair. Other evidence (Hill, 2000) has also demonstrated the earlier puberty of girls, suggesting that the average age of the onset of menstruation in Britain had dropped eight months since 1969.

In the eyes of the law

How are biological and social concepts of childhood related in contemporary society? From a legal perspective, there is considerable ambiguity about when children and young people become responsible enough to act on their own behalf. Although there are many things they can do at any age (Posner, 1995), such as opening a savings account, smoking cigarettes if they do not buy them, consenting to their own medical treatment if they can demonstrate that they understand what is involved, changing their name, suing for damages through a 'next friend' (usually a parent or guardian), being sued, carrying out odd jobs for payment, and having ears and nose pierced (although they may need to be accompanied by a parent), many activities carry age restrictions. Some of the rulings and recommendations in important areas of young people's lives are outlined below.

Definitions of childhood

There has been a shifting line as far as the legal definition of childhood is concerned. According to the 1933 Children and Young Person's Act, a child was defined as a person under 14 years and a young person as between 14 and 18 years. More recently, the Children Acts of 1989 and 2004 regard children as under the age of 18 years and do not actually define a young person. Nonetheless there are exceptions and, according to the 2001 Children (Leaving Care) Act, care leavers in full-time education can receive help for accommodation and financial support from social services until the age of 24, while the duty to remain in touch and most other supportive mechanisms operate until 21. The 1989 UN Convention on the Rights of the Child, to which the UK is a signatory, also applies to all young people under 18 (or the age of majority if earlier). Signatories agree that the courts and other public bodies will make the best interests of the child a primary consideration in all actions concerning them.

Youth justice

The current age of criminal responsibility in England and Wales is 10. Since the 1998 Crime and Disorder Act, young people have been considered to have full adult understanding of their behaviour by this age. Before this legislation, *doli incapax* had presumed that a child's understanding of right and wrong between the ages of 10 and 13 was based more on competence than age. The recent Institute for Public Policy Research Criminal Justice Report 2002, as well as the House of Lords and the House of Commons (2003) Sixth Report of the Joint Committee on Human Rights, have, however, recommended that the age of criminal responsibility is raised to 12 years, largely because criminal law is neither an appropriate response to youth offending nor effective in reducing its incidence.

It was the 1908 Children Act that effectively gave birth to the modern youth justice system as this legislation established the juvenile court (Fionda, 2001). For the 60 years or so before this date, there was a distinct move towards more child-centred and welfare-based treatment of young offenders within the adult criminal justice system. However, with the juvenile court came the recognition of childhood and the need for a distinct system of trial and punishment. Many changes have since taken place. Now, according to Fionda (2001), young people are generally regarded as competent to understand the implications of their actions and to take responsibility for them. One consequence of this view is that there are already three secure training centres for 12- to 14-year-olds in Britain as well as some 'vulnerable' 15- to 16-year-olds, and more are planned. There is at the same time an emphasis on early intervention, greater supervision and prevention, 'treatment' in the community, and bringing more agencies into the system – in theory if not fully in practice. The 2003 Anti-Social Behaviour Act, for instance, introduced new provisions, including the dispersal of groups to deal with the 'problem' of teenagers hanging around in the streets. One assumption in this Act is that the majority of anti-social behaviour is committed by young people, despite evidence to the contrary from official statistics. Responsibility for young people's behaviour is not, however, seen as theirs alone and there is an increasing push for parents to become involved and to provide control.

Education

The introduction of compulsory schooling following the 1876 Education Act helped in a sense to define childhood and the transition to independence. Although the minimum school-leaving age has changed since that time from 14 (and 10 in the case of some children living in rural areas) to 16 years, this remains true to a degree today. Nonetheless it provides only a rather rough guideline as some three quarters of young people now remain in education or training (mainly full time) beyond the period of compulsory schooling.

Children and young people are required to attend school. In general, however, the law regards parents as the primary consumer and decision maker in education in England, and they are also held responsible for a child's failure to attend school; recently, they have been successfully prosecuted in the case of persistently truant pupils. Section 176 of the 2002 Education Act has attempted to put more onus on pupils by including a clause that requires schools to consult children, but it does not carry much weight and it is the first time that consultation of this kind has been mentioned. Meanwhile, parental responsibility remains paramount in issues relating to education.

Health

A young person is recognised as an adult from 16 years for the purpose of health services and it is at this age that he or she would automatically be required to consent to treatment. This requirement was established in the 1969 Family Law Reform Act. The extension of this right to some young people under 16 was clarified by the Gillick ruling in 1985 (see pages 44–45), although this right depends on the young person being considered to have sufficient maturity and judgement to understand fully what is proposed. The more contentious issue, which is due to be resolved in a forthcoming Mental Health Bill (as yet unpublished), is a child's right to refuse treatment.

Voting

At present, young people can vote from the age of 18 years but cannot become an MP until they are 21. In April 2004, the Electoral Commission published its report on the *Age of electoral majority*, where it recommends that the voting age remain at 18, but that the age of eligibility to stand as a parliamentary candidate is reduced from 21 to 18. No decisions have, at the time of writing, been taken on these recommendations.

Age of consent

Currently, the age of consent is 16 years for both heterosexual and homosexual activities. According to the 2003 Sexual Offences Act, however, the *absolute* age of consent is 13 years. This means, theoretically, that if both 'perpetrator' and 'victim' are under 13 then both are committing a criminal act. Under 13 a young person is not capable of consenting to any sexual activity (including sexual touching, which can include kissing), and between 13 and 16 years it is a matter of 'capacity'.

There have been many changes in age of consent, even over the past 100 years. With regard to heterosexual activity, it was raised from 12 to 13 in 1875 (affecting only girls at this date), then to 16 in 1885. At the beginning of the 20th century it had, as established by the 1889 Prevention of Cruelty Act, been 14 for boys and 16 for girls. Although the NSPCC had argued for 16 for all, the gender difference was maintained on the basis that a boy of 14 was nearly independent of parents and presumed capable of looking after himself. Homosexuality was made legal from the age of 21 in 1967. This age was lowered to 18 in the 1994 Criminal Justice and Public Order Act, and to 16 in the 1999 Sexual Offences (Amendment) Act.

Alcohol and drugs

Children aged 16 or above can buy and drink certain categories of alcoholic beverage with a meal. Apart from this, no person under 18 can buy alcohol in licensed premises nor have it bought for them. There are, however, anomalies. A child of five may, for instance, drink alcohol at home, or in a registered club, provided the drink accompanies a meal and is bought by an accompanying adult.

Since January 1995 in England and Wales (and earlier in Scotland) Children's Certificates may be issued to pubs to permit them to allow accompanied children under 14 into the bars of licensed premises. The 2003 Licensing Act (due to be fully implemented by late 2005) will change the current law. One if its central principles is to protect children from harm. Section 145 therefore stipulates that accompanied children under the age of 16 may enter licensed premises. However, under-16s who are not accompanied by an adult may not.

The drugs laws reflect inconsistency and confusion. Since cannabis has been reclassified from a Class B to a Class C drug, possession of a small amount no longer represents breaking the law for anybody over 18 years. By contrast, however, young people under this age will be charged for similar behaviour. This means that, in a reverse of normal practice, young people are being treated more harshly than adults for the same act.

Employment

Current law on employment dates back to the 1933 Children and Young Persons Act. Young people under 14 should not generally work. However, if the local authority permits it, 13-year-olds can be employed on an occasional basis by their parents, or in other categories of 'light work' (such as paper rounds) if permitted by local by-laws. From the age of 14, employment must be restricted to light work for limited hours. Restrictions exist also for 15- to 18-year-olds who must, in addition, be allowed time off for study and training. In essence, therefore, the law places restrictions on employing anyone of compulsory schooling age and, according to the 2000 Children (Protection at Work) (No 2) Regulations, permits young people to work for not more than 12 hours in any week when they are required to attend school. Those under 16 may not undertake activities endangering life and limb. Updating the law in this area is currently under consideration.

The National Minimum Wage currently (since October 2004) applies to all workers aged 16 and over: 16-year-olds (who are no longer of compulsory school age) and 17-year-olds can expect to be paid at least £3 per hour, and 18- to 21-year-olds can expect at least £4.10. The standard rate for those aged 22 and over is £4.85.

The notion of 'competence' or 'capacity'

As indicated, age limits and restrictions are often accompanied by some flexibility to take into account a young person's competence and ability. This has been acknowledged explicitly since the 1985 ruling in the House of Lords in relation to *Gillick v West Norfolk and*

*Wisbech Area Health Authority.*The case in question was about the right of a girl under 16 years to medical treatment (contraception in this instance) without her parents' knowledge and consent. Lord Fraser ruled that the appropriate level of parental control depended on the child's maturity, and that the parental right to decide on such matters "terminates if and when the child achieves sufficient understanding and intelligence to enable him [or her] to understand fully what is proposed". Subsequent case law has held that 'Gillick competence' relates to a particular child and a particular treatment and, on occasion, may mean that competence is not achieved by even 16 years.

Although originally in relation to the provision of contraceptive services to young people under 16, this same principle might now be applied to GP consultations as well as consent in health areas more generally (Larchner, 2005).The principle is referred to, for instance, in Ethical Committee guidance on determining if young people decide for themselves whether or not to take part in a research enquiry.

Lewis (2001) points to evidence that a higher standard of competence is required of children than of adults. It has been suggested that not even all adults have the understanding that is expected of young people under 16 who make their own decisions. Lewis has also indicated how a young person's refusal of medical treatment, despite Gillick competence, can be overridden by consent from a person in a position of parental responsibility.

Competence in a more abstract sense has been much discussed in the sociological literature. It is seen as an essential element of childhood in which children are social actors who negotiate, and make a difference to, their own lives. Hutchby and Moran-Ellis (1998) point out how competence is not a characteristic directly related to age or which develops in a predictable, linear, developmental fashion. It is, rather, an active behaviour that is dependent on the particular structural context in which children find themselves. It is something they "negotiate, argue about and struggle over in local occasions of activity". Competencies are thus learned in a variety of settings, including the family.

At what age?

As a partial investigation of perceptions of competence, children at secondary (but not primary) schools and adults were asked four questions: at what age should young people be held legally responsible for their actions if they commit a crime (for example, shoplifting, graffiti, street crime, etc)? When should they start to learn about sex and relationships at school? When should they be able to visit their doctor on their own without a parent or other adult? When should they be allowed to baby-sit for someone else's children?

The legal position on the age of criminal responsibility has already been mentioned, as has the issue of competence in seeking medical services and support. Sex education and baby-sitting are not proscribed at specific ages although some guidance in these areas is available. There is no definite age at which sex education should begin, but DfEE (2000) guidance recommends that sex and relationships education should be a key aspect of Personal, Social and Health Education (PSHE) in primary schools, and National Curriculum Science Orders outline how sex education should be provided at all key stages. The Sex Education Forum (2002) also calls for sex and relationships education at primary level in order to support children's emotional development, prepare them for puberty, and promote self-esteem and academic achievement.

There is also no legislation on baby-sitting. The NSPCC, however, recommends that no person under 16 should be asked to baby-sit for somebody else's children. This is in line with the 1933 Children and Young Persons Act, which states that no one can be sentenced for child cruelty before the age of 16 – although the 2004 Domestic Violence, Crime and Victims Act introduced a new offence for parents of any age who are complicit in the death of their child. If a baby-sitter is less than 16, the responsibility for ensuring the care and safety of the children rests with the parents. Furthermore, children should be left in the charge of young people around 16 only if they are considered responsible enough. NSPCC guidelines recommend that most children under 13 should not be left alone for long periods.

The findings

The findings from our surveys show that secondary school children and adults broadly agreed on the ages at which young people should be permitted to do the things in question. On average, they suggested the ages shown in Figure 4.1.

Some significant differences emerged between gender and ethnicity groups. First, there were no differences between males and females in the age given for baby-sitting, but there were significant differences for the other three types of activity and responsibility (and most markedly for when young people should learn about sex). In each case males suggested a younger age. And second, there were no differences between ethnicity groups in the age given for baby-sitting,

Figure 4.1: The age at which young people should take on responsibilities. Responses by secondary school children and adults

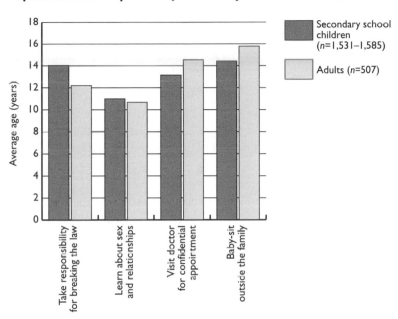

but highly significant differences in the other three areas. For each, 'White' children recommended a lower age than children from 'Other ethnicity' backgrounds.

Although, as already discussed, there are no definitive and clear-cut age boundaries in these three areas (the age of criminal responsibility at 10 years is the exception), currently recommended ages could be suggested. Starting to learn about sex could be somewhere between 7 and 11 years, visiting a doctor for a confidential consultation would at the latest be 16 years, and baby-sitting outside the family might be considered appropriate from 16 years. On this basis, the proportions of children and adults giving responses representing above, at, or below the recommended/legal age are shown in Table 4.1.

For both children and adults, the most common view was that the age of legal responsibility should be higher than it in fact is, that learning about sex and relationships should begin about when it does, and that young people should be able to visit a doctor for a confidential appointment, or baby-sit outside their family, at an age below that usually recommended. The proportions holding these attitudes varied somewhat and, overall, adults were more likely than children to agree with the generally accepted ages for responsibility and independence.

Table 4.1: Children and adults supporting ages for certain behaviours above, at or below those generally recommended

	Secondary school children (N=1,531–1,585)			Adults (N=507)		
	Recommended/ legal age			Recommended/ legal age		
	Above %	At %	Below %	Above %	At %	Below %
Take responsibility for breaking the law	86.1	8.2	3.5	64	19	16
Learn about sex and relationships	44.7	50.4	3.4	34	59	7
Visit doctor for confidential appointment	4.8	13.1	79.6	6	37	56
Baby-sit outside their family	8.6	15.4	74.2	23	35	40

Do children grow up too quickly?

Whether children are seen to grow up 'too quickly' depends on how childhood is constructed. Rousseau (1762) had quite clear ideas on this question:

> Nature wants children to be children before they are men. If we deliberately pervert this order, we shall get premature fruits which are neither ripe nor well-flavoured, and which soon decay.... Childhood has ways of seeing, thinking, and feeling peculiar to itself; nothing can be more foolish than to substitute our ways for them. (quoted in Jenks, 1996)

Much the same view motivated the reformers in the second half of the 19th century who sought to give childhood back to the children of the labouring classes. Davin (1999) comments:

> That poor children were deprived of a proper childhood, careworn and old before their time, was an increasingly frequent comment in reform circles towards the end of the century.... Children's right was to a 'natural' childhood state of innocence and irresponsibility, and any whose knowledge and responsibility were 'adult' needed rescue.

These concerns led, she says, to the support of kindergarten, child study and philanthropic projects.

Matters seem, in a sense, much more confused these days. There appears to be a widespread belief that, at one and the same time, children are being exposed to adult behaviour and culture while the disappearance of childhood is being lamented. Smith (2002) writes about this contradiction of protection and exposure and gives the example of television talent shows that encourage five-year-old children to emulate teenage and adult culture. She says:

> Like Michael Jackson before him, Declan embodies the paradox of child stars who are required to simulate adult feelings convincingly in their performances when their emotional apparatus remains that of a pre-pubescent. It is in effect an impersonation of adulthood, at an age when most children are still playing with their peers, and brings with it the twin dangers of growing up too quickly or not at all.

Lewis-Smith (2003) also points the finger at television in writing about a programme called *My Little Friends* (E4). In this, children as young as 12 years old, ask passers-by intimate questions on sex, or to spell out four letter words, "in what was a crude attempt to generate embarrassment and discomfort".

Sex, indeed, is often on the agenda in discussions about children growing up too quickly. There can, nonetheless, be something of a dilemma. An Ofsted report (2002) states that schools are good at teaching the mechanics of sex education but find it less easy to offer support in their emotional lives. According to Miles (2002):

> 'The result is that too many teenagers get the message from magazines and TV programmes that teenage sex is normal that everyone is 'at it' and that they should be too' said an Ofsted spokesperson.

Much the same might be said about joining the consumer society, as young people are being encouraged to grow up too quickly if banks allow them to have credit cards and run up thousands of pounds of debt (Revill, 2002).

While many lament the premature growing up of young people these days, there is at the same time evidence that young people often choose to delay their independence. 'Boomerang' children, who return home even after they have been away at university or elsewhere, are becoming much more common (Frean, 2002). Student debt, the high cost of housing, job instability, and relationship problems have all been blamed. A survey of 3,300 adults commissioned by BT Openworld (reported by Frean, 2002) found that 27% of leavers returned home at least once after leaving and one in ten came back four times before finally leaving. Financial considerations seemed uppermost, with only 17% of the returners saying they went back home because they missed being there. In a separate piece of research carried out by British Gas, 40% of over 1,000 16- to 24-year-olds returned home regularly for 'creature comforts'. Half said they still stored possessions at their parents' home, one in five still had mail sent there, and over half went back for home cooking.

The findings

When young people in the survey were asked whether they thought they grew up too quickly these days, the majority said 'yes'. As Figure 4.2 shows, this was the view of six in ten of the young people in contrast with fewer than two in ten who reported a definite 'no'. There was, however, a clear gender difference. In each age group girls were more likely than boys to feel that children grow up too quickly, and this was particularly marked (and statistically significant) at secondary level. Ethnicity also had an impact: children in the 'Other ethnicity' group were considerably more likely than children in the 'White' group (65% versus 56%) to say that young people grow up too quickly (Figure 4.3). This difference was maintained among males but not among females. The difference was also sustained within all age groups apart from the younger secondary school children.

Figure 4.2: Do children and young people grow up too quickly? Responses of children by age

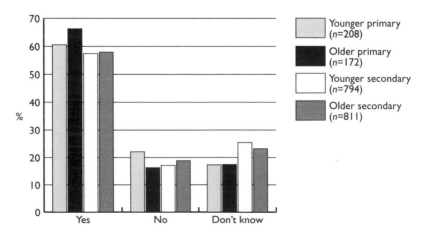

Figure 4.3: Do children and young people grow up too quickly? Responses of children by ethnicity

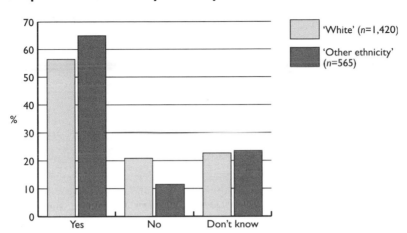

To see how far adults were in accord with young people on this matter, we asked them whether or not they agreed with the statement 'Children and teenagers have to grow up too quickly'. As shown in Figure 4.4, almost four in five agreed and just over one in ten disagreed. The main factor affecting responses was gender: 84% of women, but 72% of men, agreed that children and teenagers have to grow up too quickly these days.

Adults were also asked whether this statement is more true these days or when they were young themselves, or whether things had not really changed much. It was striking how the vast majority of adults thought that young people are much more likely to grow up 'too quickly' nowadays than in the past. Age of respondents bore no clear

Figure 4.4: Adults' responses to the statement 'Children and teenagers have to grow up too quickly' (n=507)

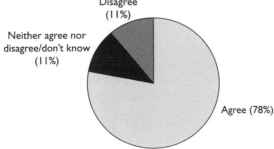

relationship to their views on this question, and gender was the strongest factor influencing responses. Overall, 80% of males but 93% of females agreed that it is truer now than in the past that young people grow up too quickly.

Making decisions

Deciding for oneself on a wide range of issues and questions is an important aspect of growing up. Nonetheless, personal autonomy depends not only on what a young person might like but also on the opportunities available. Negotiations within the family may be an important constraint even if, in the view of Giddens (1998, quoted by Langford et al, 2001), families in general are becoming more democratic:

> There is only one story to tell about the family today, and that is of democracy. The family is becoming democratised; and such democratisation suggests how family life might combine individual choice and social solidarity.... Democracy in the public sphere involves formal equality; individual rights, public discussion of issues free from violence, and authority which is negotiated rather than that given by tradition. The democratised family shares these characteristics....

It certainly does seem that children decide many things for themselves from quite a young age. This emerged from a survey that asked young people whether, at their age, they should be allowed to make certain decisions. These included hair, clothes, what they read, eat, watch on television or video, bedtimes and going out on their own (Ghate and Daniels, 1997). Not surprisingly, there was a marked difference in the responses from 8- to 11- and 12- to 15-year-olds. The main things most children felt they should decide about were hair (75% of the younger and 93% of the older children), and what they wear (71% and 91% respectively). The time they go to bed (29% and 46%), and whether they are allowed to go out on their own (23% and 47%), were things they were less likely to feel they had control over. Girls and boys expressed generally similar views, although significantly more girls thought they should make their own decisions on hairstyle while significantly more boys thought it was up to them whether or not they went out on their own. All in all, young people seemed happy with the way things were and only 12% indicated that they would like more say at home.

Increasing autonomy with age is not a surprising finding. It was also found by Langford et al (2001) who reported how parents and teenagers tend to feel their relationships become more open and less dependent on parental control over time. In many families there was no discussion between mothers and their children about teenagers' bedtimes and, certainly from 14 years, most young people made their own decisions on this matter. Getting homework done, keeping bedrooms tidy, friends, relationships with brothers and sisters, the time to be back home in the evenings, young people saying where they were going out (especially at night), finances, and appearance were, however, regarded as legitimate areas for parental concern. Young people said they expected their parents to exert authority if they did not comply.

Although research on the role of children and teenagers in family decisions has often focused on issues such as divorce proceedings or care hearings, there is a small and growing body of work that has looked at decision making at a more private level (Leach, 2003; Butler et al, 2005). Many writers have discussed how this changes over time and is affected by a tension between parental control and the young person's increasing wish for autonomy and independence. Informal negotiation, fuelled by bargaining and trade-offs, seems to characterise the process of decision making within the family. Nonetheless it appears that some family matters are more open to discussion than others, and that young people vary in their wish to participate in decisions. An interesting perspective was provided by Morrow (1998) who conducted a study with 8- to 14-year-olds. These children indicated that while they wanted a say in family matters, they did not necessarily want to make decisions. Some also explicitly recognised the difficulties that can accompany decision making within the family.

The findings

The young people in the surveys confirmed many of these findings and views. Asked whether they have to make too many decisions for themselves, most said 'yes, probably' followed by 'no, not really' (Figure 4.5). In other words, they did not feel strongly that they were required to decide too many things, but there were nonetheless decisions they would prefer not to have to make. The youngest children were most likely to think they definitely have to make too many decisions but otherwise age, gender and ethnicity did not affect views.

Figure 4.5: Do children and young people have to make too many decisions? Responses of children by age

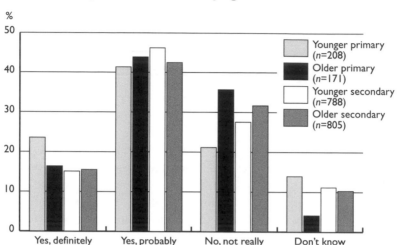

To see what adults thought, they were asked to agree or disagree with the statement that young people make too many decisions for themselves. Overall, 47% agreed, 27% disagreed, and 26% neither agreed nor disagreed (Figure 4.6). Within the sample as a whole, men, older respondents, and those from the C2 and DE social grades were most likely to agree with this statement.

Adults were also asked how far they agreed with the statement 'Young people today lead carefree lives'. Almost half thought they do, just over one third said they do not, and the rest were undecided (Figure 4.7).

There is a view that young people are more carefree these days than in the past and, as a partial test of its validity, adults were asked how far they thought things have changed in this respect since they were young.

Figure 4.6: Adults' responses to the statement 'Young people make too many decisions for themselves' (*n*=507)

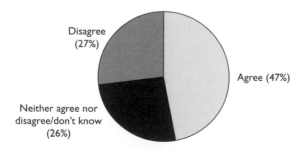

Figure 4.7: Adults' responses to the statement 'Young people today lead carefree lives' (*n*=507)

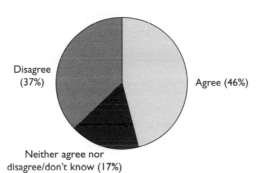

Disagree (37%)

Agree (46%)

Neither agree nor disagree/don't know (17%)

While half thought that the statement 'Young people today lead carefree lives' is more true now than in the past, almost one in three said it is less true now. Both age and social grade of respondents seemed to affect responses. The older the respondent, and the 'lower' the social grade, the more likely they were to say that young people lead more carefree lives now than in the past.

Summary

- Secondary school children and adults were in broad agreement about the ages at which children should take legal responsibility for their actions, learn about sex and relationships, be able to visit a doctor for a confidential appointment, and baby-sit outside the family.
- There were some differences in perceptions of the appropriate ages for these activities (apart from baby-sitting) according to gender and ethnicity. In each case boys tended to suggest a younger age than girls, and 'White' children suggested a younger age than children from 'Other ethnicity' backgrounds.
- Most young people thought that young people are expected to grow up too quickly these days. This was particularly true of girls as well as those from 'Other ethnicity' backgrounds.
- Adults, especially women, were in agreement that children and teenagers grow up too quickly nowadays.
- Adults saw childhood as different now from when they were young. Most, especially women, thought that young people are more likely to grow up too quickly these days. Views were more mixed on

carefree lives: half thought that young lives are more carefree these days while one in three said they are less carefree.

- Children did not seem to feel strongly that they have to make too many decisions for themselves. The younger ones were most likely to think they have to decide too much. About half the adults felt young people make too many decisions for themselves. About half also thought that young people today lead carefree lives.

"There's still a lot of old-fashioned thinking of children in the UK. So we may not be mistreating them but possibly not giving them the best upbringing." (adult)

Adults could "give us a bit more leeway with some things. But don't relax, because we do need some rules." (female, Year 7)

"When we were younger we'd go out for hours, get dirty, play cricket or rounders in the street. Kids can't do that now. Gardens are kept smart and not for playing. And the worry about letting kids out.... Everything is more organised nowadays, you just want to know where they are, who they are with, and what they are doing." (adult)

"You get a good education but it isn't always safe to go out on your own." (female, Year 7)

"I think it's discipline gone too far if you can't discipline the child. You're the parent, you're meant to be in charge." (adult)

"Not many people abuse their children and we have good human rights in this country." (male, Year 10)

"I think we've got rid of the strict control still found in developing countries but we've not gone over the top the way a few other developed countries have." (adult)

"A person of my age is like a sponge, they suck up things. They all follow each other." (male, Year 8)

"Well, I believe that because of the lack of discipline and everything else that there is in the schools and the general way they are brought up, we tend to let them rule the roost. Toys, clothes, playthings – demand and they get." (adult)

FIVE

Influences, controls and protection

Views of childhood carry implications for questions such as how much independence and control is appropriate, whether and how young people should be punished, and how far they should be protected from physical and moral dangers. These matters are affected by the cultural role and status of children and, in turn, dependent on aspects of social structure, the occupations of children, the family and the community. They also depend on perceived influences on the developing child. This chapter looks at the attitudes of children and adults towards key influences on young people, parental control, discipline and punishment, and the protection of children from physical, emotional and moral danger. First, however, there is a brief examination of some theories of child development that have, over the years, influenced approaches to child-rearing.

Models of child development

A plethora of theories about child development, which may or may not have contemporary currency, have pointed to the 'appropriate' influences, controls and forms of protection necessary to promote the optimum development of the child. What has been suggested has varied enormously and depends, for example, on whether or not behaviour and development are seen as predetermined or susceptible to external influences. The nature versus nurture debate continues and the main conclusion seems to be that genetics and the environment are both important, and that the two kinds of influence co-vary and interact. Whether there are critical or sensitive stages in human development has also been much discussed. In other words, are there specific times when experiences can have an impact, or at least ages when effects will be most marked? Many writers over the past century have based their ideas of child development on sensitive stages of some kind. Examples include Freud and Erikson in the area of emotional development, Piaget in relation to cognitive learning, and Kohlberg for moral development.

Views in these areas have, over the centuries, been reflected in the advice given in child-rearing manuals. While these give an indication of dominant attitudes and approaches to bringing up children at various points in history, they do not necessarily reflect how most children were actually brought up. Historians tend to use these manuals as sourcebooks of ideologies and practice but it is not always clear how far they illustrate common patterns and trends. Certainly they do say something about attitudes to childhood, and highlight how starkly views from one period contrasted with those of another. They have ranged from punitive to liberal, from oppressive to sensitive. Puritanism in the 16th century, for example, provides a good example of a strict regime. Advocates believed that every child was born with 'original sin' that had to be brought under control and eliminated. Upbringing was harsh, as urged by John Hersey, a New England minister:

> Break their will betimes…. Begin the work before they can run, before they can speak plainly or speak at all. Whatever pains it costs, conquer their stubbornness; break their wills if you will not damage the child. Therefore let a child from a year old be taught to fear the rod and cry softly. Make him do as he is bid if you whip him ten times running to do it; let none persuade you that it is cruel to do this. (quoted in de Mause, 1976)

Attitudes had mellowed by the mid to late 18th century when parents were being advised to treat their children more sensitively and considerately. And, as Hardyment (1983) points out, by the beginning of the 19th century children were being "seen as little animals, puppies rather than plants". Training was to lead to good habits and:

> What was new was to base training on a structure derived from neurology and psychology rather than the old one of physiology and religion. It took a lot of the heat out of nurture once original sin was replaced by inherited weakness. Parents could hardly blame their children for faults they had passed down to them themselves.

The trend towards more considerate treatment of children continued, and Hardyment (1983) notes how between 1820-70 extreme oppression of children for their own good was not a typical approach. It was no longer felt that getting rid of evil before good could be substituted, or breaking natural will, was appropriate, and indeed Mrs Ellis (1843) had illustrated how such approaches had not resulted in 'better' adults. Instead, she and other contemporaries regarded the parent as some kind of gardener whose role was "to stake up deserving mental qualities and weed out those that were undesirable".

Since then there have been further shifts in attitudes to children. The general direction has been towards acknowledging their individuality, understanding their physical and emotional needs, offering increased rights and protection through legislation and reform. Interest in children's development and well-being has soared, as has the study of childhood as a subject in itself. Darwin contributed to this trend by publishing a detailed account of the early months of one of his own children in 1877. This was followed by the Child Study Movement with the formation of Child Study Associations and the introduction of specialist journals. The British Child Study Association was founded in 1894, and the Childhood Society and the Parents' National Educational Union (PNEU) soon followed. The feeling of the time was that parents should observe their own children as much as possible so that the scientific study of childhood could progress. The general view was that careful upbringing could modify the impact of heredity, but that it was necessary to appreciate the important influences on development. The investigation of childhood has not looked back.

Families, friends and the media

Turning to the present, current understanding of childhood places considerable emphasis on the role of experience. The culture children grow up in, the opportunities they receive, the disadvantages and abuse they may suffer, the quality of their relationships with parents and friends, and many other aspects of their day-to-day lives, are thought to influence their well-being and behaviour. Their vulnerabilities, but also the aspects of their lives that appear to offer them protection against adverse circumstances, are accordingly of particular interest.

The role of parents, families, friends and the media in affecting children's and young people's ideas and views is much discussed. There is strong evidence to support the significance of families during the child's transition to adulthood. Despite some suggestion (for example, Fenwick and Smith, 1993) that children grow away from their parents as they pass through adolescence, families continue to be an important source of support for most young people. Madge and Franklin's (2003) survey of almost 3,000 secondary school children in two areas of England found that parents, and then friends, emerged as preferred sources of support almost whatever the problem. Parents were mentioned in particular for help with friendships, school problems and stress, and minor illnesses, while friends were of prime importance for help over relationships with parents.

Balding (2002) found much the same. Parents, particularly mothers, came out top for providing young people with information on sex and help with problems relating to school, money, health and career. Friends, nonetheless, were a main source of information about sex (television and films seemed important for males, while magazines were more important for females). Friends were also important confidants for school problems, difficulties with friends and, for females, family problems.

A BT/ChildLine (2002) study also found that young people see parents/guardians as the most important source of information – and more important than adults realise. Friends were second most important, and the media third. The media were, however, more significant for young people than adults appreciated and this applied to television news (39% of young people but 23% of adults thought this was important), newspapers (37% compared with 21%), and radio (35% and 20%). The study also found that, as they get older, children and young people turn increasingly to friends and media channels for information.

There has always been more belief in the power of the media to influence children than evidence to support the belief. Research carried out over the years has attempted to 'prove' effects of the media on a range of behaviour from violence and suicide to sexuality and consumerism, but conclusions remain elusive (for example, Ericson, 1995; Kidd-Hewitt and Osborne, 1995; Barker and Petley, 1997). This is hardly surprising given the variability of the evidence and, often, its tangential relationship to the question under investigation. Studies, for instance, may be based on laboratory situations that in no way reflect the reality – for example, watching a cartoon film in which one plant attacks another, and then judging induced aggression in children by the number of balloons they pop afterwards.

The 'golden question', says Howitt (1998), is whether violence in the media can lead to criminal or deviant behaviour. Even if the 10-year-old boys who killed James Bulger had watched video nasties shortly before the murder, this does not necessarily mean the videos *caused* it. Brown (2003) talks about the 'effects debate', illustrates its futility, and points out how Barker and Petley (1997):

> ... examine the much more fascinating question of the insistence of political and moral interest groups, and

ironically the media itself, on centralizing a question which has so palpably refused to be answered.

Buckingham (2000) enters the debate and points to different views on the role of the media in influencing constructions of childhood. From one perspective, television and other media have erased the boundaries between childhood and adulthood and contributed to the death of childhood. From another, however, new media technologies have increased the distance between children and adults and thereby reinforced the division between the generations. Buckingham believes that the electronic media, as an aspect of culture and representation, play a significant role in developing and sustaining contemporary constructions of childhood.

There are, in addition, real concerns about some of the more immediate effects of the media on young people. Hastings et al (2003) suggest links between advertisements for food and drink and child obesity. And there is some evidence to indicate that cigarette advertising may encourage young people to start smoking. Balding (2002) asked young people (12 to 15–year–old males and females) what they thought on this issue, and most seemed to think that advertising had some effect of this kind. Males tended to be more extreme in their views, either for or against, and younger pupils were more likely than older pupils to regard advertising as powerful in this way. Parents, too, may feel that advertising affects their children. The National Family and Parenting Institute (NFPI) (2003) published MORI research showing that parents point to commercial pressure on their children as the most difficult part of their parenting role.

The findings

The children, teenagers and adults in the study were asked for their views on the strongest influences on children's and young people's ideas and views. Primary school children were asked 'Where do children get most of their ideas from?' and ranked their first, second and third choices from the options of parents, brothers and sisters, television, friends, teachers, magazines and books, and something else. At secondary level, children were asked 'Which of the following do you think have the strongest influence on the views of young people of your age?' and selected their top three choices from the same options. Adults were asked 'Which do you think has the strongest influence on children and teenagers today?' from the possibilities of media, friends/peer pressure, family/parents, or none of these.

The views of children and adults were very different (Figure 5.1). Children said they were influenced most by their parents and families, but adults thought that friends and peer pressure were more important. The two generations may have had different things in mind when answering this question, but it does seem that young people think of their parents and families as much more important and influential than adults themselves realise – even if parents were more likely than non-parents to think family and parents are a strong influence. On the whole, adults attributed much more importance to friends and peers than young people did. Secondary school children, however, were most likely to highlight the importance of friends, and the influence of peers clearly increases with age.

Age also affects views on the role of the media. In line with other research findings, the relative influence of the media (defined as television, books and magazines for the children and young people) and friends changes as children move from primary to secondary school level. Overall, young people and adults felt similarly about the influence of the media on children and teenagers.

Figure 5.1: The strongest influences on children and young people. Responses of children and adults

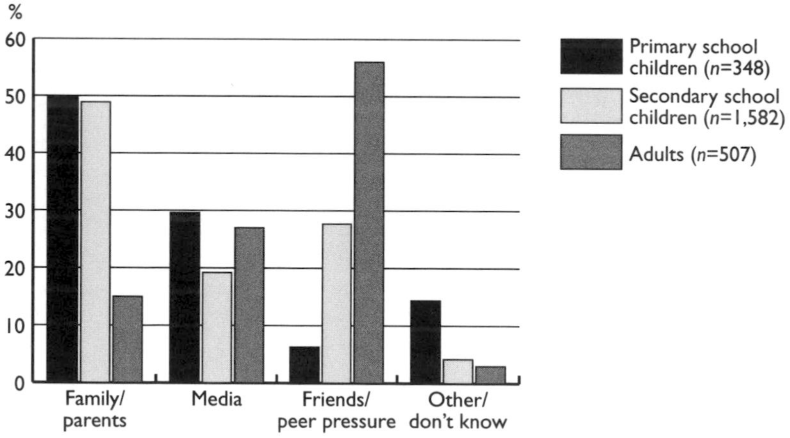

Adults' views on young people's behaviour

Some influences on children's behaviour involve parental control. To find out what adults think about this, they were first asked whether parents adequately control their young children in public places. Almost seven in ten adults said they do not, but responses were affected by age: while 49% of adults aged 20 to 34 years agreed with this statement, the proportion rose to 82% of those aged 55 years or more (Figure 5.2).

Figure 5.2: Adults' responses to the statement 'Parents do not adequately control their young children in public places' (n=507)

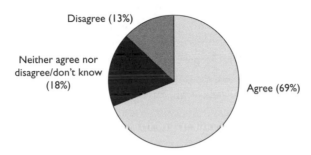

Disagree (13%)

Neither agree nor disagree/don't know (18%)

Agree (69%)

Adults were next asked the broader question of whether children's and young people's behaviour is controlled strictly enough. Almost eight in ten, particularly older and male respondents, said that it is not (Figure 5.3).

Figure 5.3: Adults' responses to the statement 'Children's and teenagers' behaviour is not controlled strictly enough' (n=507)

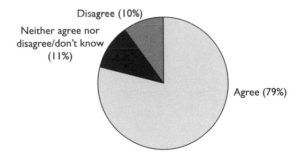

Disagree (10%)

Neither agree nor disagree/don't know (11%)

Agree (79%)

Discipline and punishment

Discipline and punishment may be seen as important ways of influencing and controlling children and their behaviour. Attitudes have, however, wavered and Tomison (2001) discusses how approaches to child protection have gone round in circles over the past 150 years or so. He also points out how committed opponents of physical punishment have always existed, and mentions Plato's entreaties as long ago as 400 BC as well as a book by Roger L'Estrange in the seventeenth century imploring parents to treat their children more leniently.

These days we formally outlaw physical punishment yet implicitly acknowledge its existence. In 2003, corporal punishment was finally banned in all schools across the UK, and by all childcare providers including childminders, day care providers, nannies and au pairs. And only in 2004 were restrictions imposed on the use of the defence of 'reasonable chastisement' for parents disciplining their children at home. Nonetheless, a considerable proportion of parents report using some form of physical punishment at least occasionally. A survey of parental discipline in Britain (Ghate et al, 2003), carried out before the latest legislation, found that over half the nationally representative sample of 1,250 parents with children up to the age of 12 (Ghate et al, 2003) said they had used minor physical punishment, such as smacking and slapping, over the past year, and almost one in ten said they had used severe forms of physical punishment. These acts of discipline were generally administered alongside non-physical means of punishment. Most parents, however, either rejected physical punishment altogether or found it acceptable only in certain circumstances – most commonly, to prevent a child from doing something dangerous. Almost all parents disapproved of severe methods of discipline such as hitting a child with an implement. Younger children were most likely to be smacked, and parents who were young or had unsupportive parents were most likely to smack.

Cawson (2002) reports on young people's views of discipline and portrays a similar picture. Almost nine in ten young people said that any discipline they had received was usually based on reasoning, explanation and other forms of non-physical punishment. Overall, three quarters said they had been grounded or sent to their room. When they had been physically punished, this was described in three out of four cases as mild and infrequent.

Perhaps surprisingly, young people often emerge as firm supporters of discipline and control. Smith (2003) concludes that:

> A picture seems to be emerging that portrays young people as generally sharing many of the moral judgements of the community in general, expressing similar concerns about personal safety and the fear of crime, and holding similar views about the need for tighter control and tough punishment.

Evidence for this conclusion comes from a variety of sources. The Children and Young People's Unit (CYPU, 2001) reports how consultations with young people provide some support for the view that young people do believe in tough punishment. It gives the example of a 12-year-old boy who said "if somebody is caught they should be punished severely". At the same time, however, Willow (1999) suggests that young people may also be particularly understanding of the reasons why others of their age might commit crimes and think they should be treated leniently. She quotes a young person who says:

'Some people in gangs get involved because they could have a bad life at home, and ... [they're] pressured into it. That's how people join gangs, they're pressured into it. Having a lot of trouble at home and that.'

An exploration of views on smacking carried out by young people with other young people (NCB, 2004) reported that many children were in favour of a ban on corporal punishment even though some had worries about how such a ban might work. If evidence from Germany is anything to go by, such a ban in Britain might well lead to less physical discipline and general acceptance of the prohibition (Bussmann, 2004). In thinking about the pros and cons of legislation of this kind, an interesting question might be whether patterns of discipline affect later attitudes and behaviour. Adult recollections of over 1,000 adults in England, Wales and Scotland suggest they might (Creighton and Russell, 1995). Those who reported little or no physical punishment as children said they brought up their children in a similar way. However, those who reported frequent punishment themselves said they were more tolerant than their own parents, but nonetheless punished their own children more than those brought up more leniently.

The findings

What did the young people in the study think? Asked how strict their own childhoods were, the most typical responses were 'quite strict' or 'not very strict'. Fewer than one in ten reported a 'very strict' upbringing and, despite no sex differences overall, primary age boys were twice as likely as girls to say their parents were very strict (13% and 7% respectively) (Figure 5.4). There was also a tendency for 'Other ethnicity' children to be more likely than 'White' children to say they were brought up strictly (Figure 5.5).

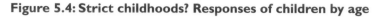

Figure 5.4: Strict childhoods? Responses of children by age

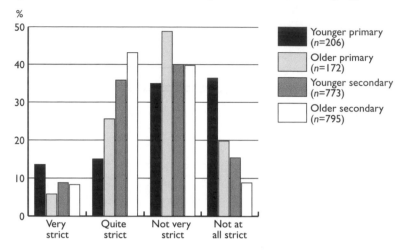

Figure 5.5: Strict childhoods? Responses of children by ethnicity

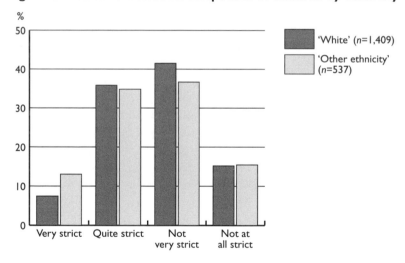

Adults were asked similar questions about their own childhoods and, as might be expected, said that parents are less strict these days than in the past. Overall, 70% said their own childhood had been very strict (26%) or quite strict (44%) and 10% said it had been quite lenient (8%) or very lenient (2%). The remaining one in five thought it had been neither strict nor lenient. No clear differences according to age (although those in the 20-34 year-old group were least likely to say they had been brought up strictly), or gender, were found.

Finally, we asked adults for their views on smacking. More than four in five thought parents should be allowed to decide whether or not to smack their own children (Figure 5.6). Those aged 55 years or more, and men without children or teenagers of their own, were most likely to hold this view.

Figure 5.6: Adults' responses to the statement 'Parents should be allowed to decide whether to smack their children' (*n*=507)

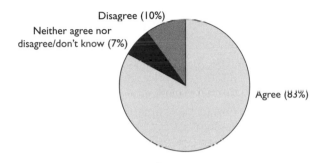

Disagree (10%)

Neither agree nor disagree/don't know (7%)

Agree (83%)

A dangerous environment?

Young people need protection from many potential hazards and dangers in the environment but, as Furedi (2001) asks, have we now become paranoid parents? In his view:

> We live in a climate of permanent panic that invites a guilt-ridden style of parenting.

He argues that even though children are far less vulnerable now than a century or even 30 years ago, children are allowed to take fewer and fewer risks. Moorcock (1998) notes an abundance of information for parents and carers on the possible dangers that abound yet little information on the actual risks involved.

Staying safe is one of the five outcomes for children outlined in *Every child matters* as of primary concern for children and young people (DfES, 2003). Physical protection of children is also a high priority for parents. Scott et al (2000), for example, found that parents feel under increasing pressure to ensure their children's safety from such things as traffic, strangers and drugs, and McNeish and Roberts (1995) report that parents are most worried about stranger danger, followed by traffic and drugs.

Concepts of safety and danger, as well as their implications, however, differ for children and their parents (Borland et al, 1998). Adult perceptions of danger can mean that children ready for independence are nowadays denied it (Hillman et al, 1990; Ball, 1998), and result in Britain's parks and playgrounds becoming 'boring' as activities carrying even the slightest risk of injury are banned (The Children's Society and the Children's Play Council, 2002). A survey of 500 young people found many were not allowed to ride bicycles or skateboards, climb trees or climbing frames, or play with water. At school they were also being prevented from playing tag, doing handstands, playing with yoyos and making daisy chains.

Taking risks is normal (Essau, 2004), and central to an understanding of childhood and adolescence (Mitchell et al, 2004). What children are allowed and encouraged to do is a direct reflection of social and cultural concepts of childhood. McKendrick et al (2000) are among those who say that concern for child safety has gone too far with "detrimental implications for children's physical and personal development". Lindon (1999) also argues that over-protecting children will not "enable them to emerge as competent and confident adults". What do children themselves think?

So, are parents over-protective?

Young people in the survey were asked whether they thought parents and carers 'over-protect' children and young people of their age. Over three quarters at primary school level said adults worry too much about them hurting themselves or being in danger. A further 15% said this was 'sometimes' the case, and only one in 20 said it was 'not very often' true (Figure 5.7). Girls were slightly more likely to see themselves as over-protected in this sense.

Figure 5.7: Do parents or carers worry too much about you hurting yourself or being in danger? Responses of primary school children (n=377)

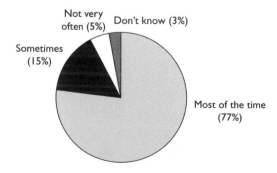

Older children were asked the more general question of whether parents and carers over-protect their children. Overall, 41% said that 'most do', 49% said that 'some do and some don't', and only 7% said 'most don't'. As shown in Figure 5.8, girls were more likely than boys to think parents and carers are over-protective.

Overall, 47% of adults agreed with the statement 'Parents over-protect their children', 29% disagreed, and 24% neither agreed nor disagreed, or did not know (Figure 5.9). Non-parents, those in the youngest age band, and those from C2 and DE social grades, were least likely to agree.

Figure 5.8: Do parents and carers over-protect their children? Responses of secondary school children by gender

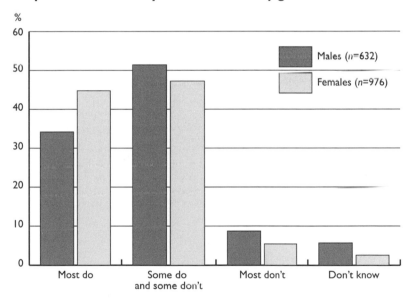

Figure 5.9: Adults' responses to with the statement 'Parents over-protect their children' (n=507)

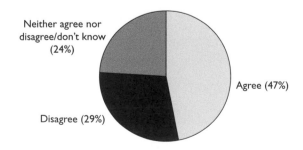

Have things changed?

To find out how far things may have changed, adults were asked if they thought parents protect their children more nowadays than in the past. Well over half (56%) thought more now, and these were more likely to be parents than non-parents, and particularly fathers. Non-parents in contact with children or young people were also more likely to take this view than non-parents without such contact. Fewer than a quarter of the adults overall felt that parents protected their children more in the past.

Summary

- Young people and adults had different views about the main influences on children. While children pointed to parents and families as most important, adults mentioned friends and peer pressure. Young people did indicate, nonetheless, that the influence of peers increases with age.
- The majority of adults, particularly the oldest in the sample, did not think that adults adequately control their young children in public places. They also felt more generally, that children's and young people's behaviour is not controlled strictly enough.
- Fewer than one in ten children regarded their childhood as very strict. Primary school boys and children from 'Other ethnicity' backgrounds were among those most likely to feel they are being brought up strictly.
- By contrast, seven in ten adults reported that their own childhoods had been either very or quite strict.
- More than four in five adults, especially those who were older and men without children or teenagers of their own, thought parents should be allowed to decide whether or not to smack their own children.
- Over three quarters of primary school children said that adults regularly worry about them hurting themselves or being in danger. Four in ten at secondary level felt that parents and carers are over-protective.
- Almost half the adults agreed that young people are over-protected these days.

"

"Older people are not always polite to younger people. I fell in the precinct and there were three students who came to help me. I find them pleasant, except for in a group." (adult)

"Well [children] seem to argue more with their parents than families abroad. They have a little less respect for them." (adult)

"Some adults think we are just children so we should be treated with not as much respect as adults." (female, Year 6)

"Children could show more respect to gain it back in return." (female, Year 10)

"I get the feeling parents aren't very good at being parents and the result of that is lack of respect of children towards their seniors." (adult)

"

SIX

Status and respect

The status of children, their role within their families, what the generations think of each other, and how far young people's views and wishes are valued and tolerated, are among the questions examined in this chapter. First, however, the meaning of parenthood for adults, and young people's views on parents, are explored briefly.

The meaning of parenthood

The status of childhood depends on the meaning of parenthood for adults. Why do people have children, and what expectations do they have of them?

Views of children have changed considerably over the years. These reflect both social climate and adult lifestyles. By way of illustration, Hardyment (1983) tells how between about 1820 and 1870, children were regarded with great affection and tolerance, and as a hope for the future. Towards the end of this period, however, important changes took place. Women were developing their social roles and had less time to devote to raising large families. Birth control became more widespread, and family size declined dramatically. Nurses and nannies took over in families who could afford them, and fewer childcare manuals were written for parents. By the 20th century, or the 'century of the child' as Hardyment calls it, things changed again. More texts than ever appeared on bringing up babies:

> Medical, scientific and political developments combined
> at the turn of the century to turn a floodlight of interest
> and anticipation on the small creatures hitherto left to
> tumble up together in their nurseries.

Throughout the centuries, for a variety of reasons, children have been seen as an asset. They have been valued for their ability to earn extra money for the family – even if this is a far cry from the more common view these days about how costly children and young people are (Middleton et al, 1997). Historically, they have been regarded as property, with parents even having the right to sell their own children for slavery, or worse. Freeman (2001) comments on how the 1989 Children Act finally eliminated the old idea of the 'ownership' of children:

> The significance of the reconstruction of the parent–child relationship as based on parental responsibility rather than the traditional parental rights must also not be overlooked. Rights are redolent of the ties between a person and property, whereas responsibilities suggest more the relationship between a trustee and the beneficiary of that trust. Children are reconceptualised as persons and thus as participants in the social process rather than as possessions or problems.

These days many parents have children for much more 'emotional' reasons. A recent study of the role of children in families reported by Stanley et al (2003), and based on eight focus groups and a survey of 1,500 men and women aged between 20 and 40 across Britain, suggests that many people become parents to make them happy. It was found that most adults wanted, or had, children and only 11% of those in their 20s, and 9% in their 30s, explicitly said they did not want any. Asked 'what gives you most happiness in your life?', 66% of mothers and 41% of fathers said their children did. Fathers, nonetheless, were likely to say that 'family and friends' were most important overall.

Parents also acknowledged that their children were a challenge and could make them unhappy. Fathers in particular mentioned the difficulties of parenting, while mothers were more likely to highlight the effects of children on their career as well as on their status in society. Children could also be hurtful and make parents feel guilty.

The World Values Survey (2001) (see Stanley et al, 2003) suggested that people do not define their personal fulfilment only in terms of their children. Indeed fewer than 12% of British women, and only 20% of British men, thought it was necessary for a woman to have children for her to feel fulfilled. McAllister and Clarke (1998) also demonstrated that a growing number of adults remain voluntarily childless.

The positive aspects of parenthood were examined by Langford et al (2001) who interviewed parents of teenagers. These told how their children made them feel part of a group and gave them pleasure and emotional fulfilment. They also liked being 'grown-up' in relation to dependent children so that they could gain gratification 'through demonstrating adult competencies such as caring, providing, helping and advising'. In addition, they felt they could identify with their developing teenagers, their talents and potential, and could make up for any past tensions by becoming involved in their children's school activities and encouraging them to do well. They looked back on family life and its 'togetherness' with nostalgia.

Children's views on their parents

Children also have views on their parents and the parenting role. While they do not all describe families in the same way or agree about the meaning of a 'proper family' (Brannen et al, 2000), they are generally agreed that what they most want from parents is to be loved and cared for, listened to, taken seriously and valued (Borland et al, 1998; Montandon, 2001). There is also widespread consensus that they rely on parents, especially mothers, for providing support, information and advice (Madge and Franklin, 2003; SHEU, 2005). This seems as true of 6- to 9-year-olds (Cullingford, 1997) as of 18- to 24-year-olds (Cawson, 2002). Young people may, in this sense, be becoming more reliant on parents than in the past (SHEU, 2005).

Mothers and fathers do, however, tend to be viewed rather differently. They are seen as having distinct gendered responsibilities (Mayall, 2001), and children seem to regard only family finances and discipline as the tasks fathers are usually expected to undertake (NCH Action for Children, 1997). As fathers are less likely to live with their children than mothers, this can also affect their role within the family in broader ways (Flouri et al, 2004).

There is no doubt that, in the vast majority of cases, parents and families are of central significance in children's lives (NFPI, 2000). Evidence on the quality of their relationships, and the impact these may have, is discussed further in Chapter Seven.

Is respect mutual?

Parents may want children, and children may appreciate their parents, but how far do the generations appear to respect each other? Young people and adults were asked for their opinions. Those at primary school were asked whether children their age are polite enough to adults and whether adults are polite enough to the children. Secondary school children were asked whether the generations show enough respect for each other. Adults were asked whether they agreed with the statements 'Children and teenagers show enough respect for adults' and 'Adults show enough respect for children and teenagers'.

The views of children and adults were remarkably similar (Figures 6.1, 6.2 and 6.3). All groups seemed to agree that adults are more polite and respectful to children than children are to adults. There were also some interesting differences within the groups, such as between boys and girls at primary level. Boys of this age were less likely to think that children are polite enough to adults and more likely to say they 'don't know'. There were also striking differences according to age with the younger primary school children almost twice as likely as the older children to think they are polite enough. Ethnicity did not make a difference to their views.

The age of primary school children also made a difference to whether or not they thought *adults* are polite enough although it had less impact than on their views about whether children are polite enough. The younger children were, the more often they said that adults are polite enough to children of their age. There was, in addition, a link between ethnicity and attitudes in that 'White' children were more likely than 'Other ethnicity' children to report that most adults are polite enough to children.

Age, gender and ethnicity made little difference to secondary school children's views about the respect young people of their age show for adults, and age was the only factor influencing their views on the respect adults pay them. The younger secondary children were well

Figure 6.1: Are children and adults polite enough to each other? Responses of primary school children (*n*=380)

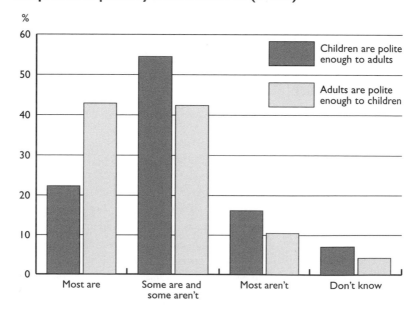

Figure 6.2: Do young people of your age and adults show enough respect for each other? Responses of secondary school children (*n*=1,632/1,624)

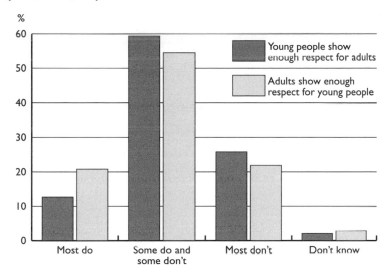

Figure 6.3: Do children and teenagers, and adults, show enough respect for each other? Responses of adults (*n*=507)

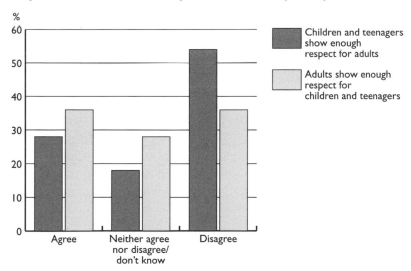

over twice as likely as the older group to think adults show young people enough respect.

Adults were asked whether they agreed, disagreed, neither agreed nor disagreed, or did not know, with the following two statements, 'Children and teenagers show enough respect for adults' and 'Adults show enough respect for children and teenagers'. Their views mirrored those of the young people in that they, too, thought that adults are more respectful than children and teenagers. Indeed, while they were about as likely to agree or disagree with the statement that adults show enough respect for children and teenagers, they were considerably more likely to disagree than agree that children and teenagers show enough respect for adults.

Taking children's and young people's views into account

Recent years have seen a marked change in expectations about how far young people should play a part in decisions that affect their lives. These might be on matters affecting them personally (for example, living arrangements after their parents' divorce), local provision (for example, the facilities of a local park), or national policies (for example, the age at which young people can vote). The consensus these days is that young people should be involved in decision making not least because they are competent to do so (Alderson, 1993; Clark and Moss, 2001; Willow et al, 2003). Young people are also in the best position to make judgements for themselves and, as young citizens, have rights as well as everyone else. The argument is that encouraging children's participation empowers them, increases their skills and knowledge, and raises their self-esteem.

These arguments have long been recognised, if only by some. As far back as 1840 Andrew Coombe (quoted by Hardyment, 1983) wrote:

> Adaptation to the wants, feelings and nature of the infant –
> so different in many ways from those of the adult – ought
> to be made the leading principle of our management ...
> accordingly the child ought as far as possible to be allowed
> the choice of its own occupations and amusements and to
> become the chief agent in the development and formation
> of its own character. In later life, the independent child
> will show far more promptitude and energy than the
> 'puppet' dominated by parents and trained in moral slavery.

Unfortunately this has not been the dominant view historically.

In more modern times, the ratification of the UN Convention on the Rights of the Child by the UK government in 1991 has encouraged and reinforced the movement towards greater involvement of children in decision making. Article 12 is particularly significant in stating that all children have the right to express their views and have them taken seriously. The 1989 Children Act has also played a role, even if it did not go as far as later guidance, in outlining how children are entitled to have a say, although not necessarily the final say, in matters affecting them. Additionally, each nation in the UK has appointed a statutory Children's Commissioner. These posts were established in Wales in March 2001, in Northern Ireland in October 2003, in Scotland in April 2004, and in England in March 2005. One of the main functions of this role is to listen to, represent, and respond to the views of children and young people.

So, children's participation these days is firmly on the agenda. The Children's and Young People's Unit (CYPU, 2001) outlined how:

> The Government wants children and young people to have more opportunities to get involved in the design, provision and evaluation of policies and services that affect them or which they use.

Government departments are responding to the challenge, as are a wide range of organisations, services, initiatives and activities. There are numerous demonstrations nowadays of how models of participation are being, and can be, implemented (for example, Kirby et al, 2003; Mason and Fattore, 2005) to be "meaningful, effective and sustainable" (Sinclair, 2004). Participation has also become a key element of many new national frameworks for youth action (for example, Russell, 2005).

Principle and practice do not, however, always proceed hand-in-hand, and it is interesting to see how far young people feel their views are taken into account. Some evidence comes from a qualitative and quantitative study with 5- to 16-year-olds across the UK commissioned by BT and ChildLine (2002). This sought to establish whether children and young people felt they have a voice in society, and it collected complementary information from adults. In all, some 1,400 young people and 1,500 adults took part.

Several interesting findings emerged. One was a discrepancy between the numbers of young people and adults who strongly agreed that young people have the right to say what they think. Six in ten young people, but fewer than half this proportion of adults, took this view. There was more agreement about whether adults listen to young people and act on what they hear, with 47% of young people and 57% of adults saying that they do. The young people also said they most wanted to have a say about how schools could improve things, how to have more fun as a family, how the council could improve local services, and how police treat young people.

The findings

Children and young people in the sample were asked how often their parents and carers listen to what they think and take their views into account. Just under half the children felt their viewpoint was heeded most of the time but, as can be seen from Figure 6.4, the younger ones were most likely to think this was the case. Neither gender nor ethnicity seemed to make much difference to responses.

Are young people listened to more than in the past? Adults' attitudes were sought by asking them whether the views of young people are taken into account more, less or about the same nowadays as compared with when they were young. Over two thirds gave the impression that young people are consulted much more these days. Only 13% said young people's views are taken into account less now than in the past and 18% said things have not changed much (Figure 6.5).

Adults were not, however, complacent. Well over half agreed that children's and teenagers' ideas and opinions are not valued highly enough, and this was particularly true of parents. The majority (over seven in ten) also agreed that adults can learn a lot from children and teenagers. These were especially likely to be women and adults from AB and C1 social grades.

Figure 6.4: How often do parents and carers listen to what you think/take your views into account? Responses of children by age

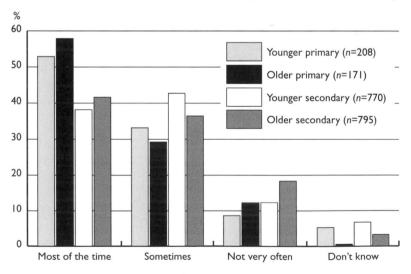

Figure 6.5: Adults' responses on how often their views were taken into account when they were young (*n*=507)

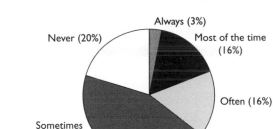

Adults' tolerance of young people's clothes and hairstyles

Choosing clothes and hairstyles is an everyday matter where adults may try to intervene in children's and young people's decision making, and primary school children in the survey were asked whether or not this happened. Well over half said their parents and carers did let them choose their own clothes and hairstyle (Figure 6.6). There was a statistically significant difference between boys and girls, with girls given a greater degree of autonomy. Age and ethnicity did not seem to affect patterns.

Figure 6.6: Do your parents or carers let you choose your own clothes and hairstyles? Responses of primary school children by gender

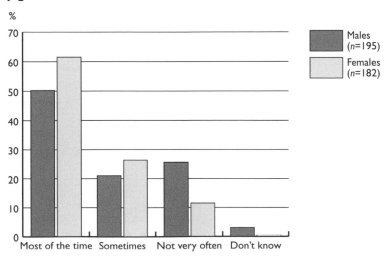

Secondary school children were instead asked whether adults are tolerant of young people's clothes and hairstyles. Fewer than a quarter thought they were, and half said that while some were, others were not (Figure 6.7). Age made a difference and younger children were most likely to say 'most are'. Ethnicity did not affect responses.

Adults were also asked for their views: did they agree or disagree with the statement that 'Adults are tolerant of young people's clothes and hairstyles'? In all, 54% agreed and 25% disagreed. The remaining 21% neither agreed nor disagreed or did not know. Age seemed to have no bearing, but parents were marginally more likely than non-parents to think that adults are generally tolerant in this area.

Summary

- Children and adults agreed that adults are more polite and respectful to young people than children are to adults.
- 'White' primary school level children were more likely than children from 'Other ethnicity' backgrounds to think that adults are polite to children of their age.
- Age at secondary school level affected young people's views on the respect they received from adults: the younger group was over twice as likely as the older group to feel young people are shown enough respect.

Figure 6.7: Are adults tolerant of young people's clothes and hairstyles? Responses of secondary school children by gender

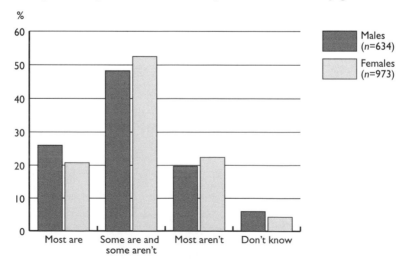

- Almost half the children thought that parents and carers listen to their views and take them into account most of the time.
- Over two in three adults felt that children's views are taken into account more now than when they were young.
- Over half the adults, especially parents, thought that children's and teenagers' ideas and opinions are not valued highly enough. Most also agree that adults can learn a lot from children and teenagers.
- Half the children at primary school level said they choose their own clothes and hairstyles. Fewer than a quarter of those at secondary school level said that most adults are tolerant of young people's clothes and hairstyles, although a further half thought some were and some were not.
- Over half the adults regarded adults as tolerant of young people's clothes and hairstyles.

"Most parents think their child is an angel – it's other kids who corrupt them." (adult participant in focus group: non-parent, 20-34 years)

"We are probably only friendly to our own children." (adult)

Adults could "listen more and understand what it would be like to be in their shoes, because they were a child once and they wouldn't like getting told off." (female, Year 5)

"Children could listen to what adults say as they are often right even though we don't always want to believe it." (female, Year 10)

Children should "learn not to take things to heart. Work with your parents and love them and yourself." (male, Year 7)

"Adults could listen to what children say and their views. Not take over our lives too much. Let us make most of our own decisions." (male, Year 7)

"I think that we are always having a go at teenagers." (adult)

"Not many people like children enough." (adult)

SEVEN

Getting along together

The degree of contact between adults and young people, the nature of that contact, the quality of parent–child relationships, and whether adults think differently about their own and other people's children, all contribute to how the generations get along together. This chapter focuses on the things young people do with their parents and carers, and the extent to which the generations feel they talk and listen to each other. Some comparisons are drawn between adults' attitudes to their own children and to children in general.

A context of unease

Relationships between the generations are not independent of society and its pressures. This chapter begins by considering some of the ways in which these relationships have become more self-conscious than in the past and the impact this can have.

Much of the tension contributing to uneasy relationships across the generations can be traced to concerns about protecting young people from dangerous situations. Well-publicised and horrific cases of physical and sexual abuse have pinpointed child protection as a matter of high priority and led to increased monitoring of professions in contact with young people, thorough vetting and police checks by the Criminal Records Bureau, improved recruitment and training, and many other linked measures. These actions, as well as the heightened awareness of child maltreatment, have nonetheless engendered a certain anxiety within the wider community. Many adults these days are loath to assist or talk to a child in a public place, just as children are often reluctant to speak to unknown adults as they heed persistent warnings of 'stranger danger'. At the extreme, even smiling at a child, or helping a young person to cross the road, could be misconstrued. Similar issues can arise in settings such as schools where teachers and others realise that young people may be 'streetwise' enough to make false allegations against them. The fear of accidental injury and the possibility of consequent litigation is another factor that can curtail interactions between adults and young people in a variety of settings including schools and clubs.

Anxieties may also occur within the family. Parents have been apprehended for photographs they have taken of their unclothed young children, and many will privately admit to worrying about their quite normal physical contact with their own children. Parents may also feel insecure in their relationships with their children for other reasons – fathers, in particular, especially if they are not married to the mother and/or have left the family home, may have restricted rights. The encouragement of more fathers to sign a Parental Responsibility Agreement has, however, improved this position.

Patterns of contact between adults, children and young people

All children come into contact with adults – as parents and carers, teachers, medical practitioners, neighbours, shopkeepers and in many other roles – but how many adults come into regular one-to-one contact with children and young people? The evidence from the adult survey suggests the answer is most.

At the time of the survey, 42% of the sample (86 men and 127 women) had children under 20 years living with them and 58% (160 men and 133 women) did not. A further 27 members of the sample (16 men and 11 women) had children under 20 years who did not live with them. Of these non-residing children, three were aged 5 years or less, 11 were between 6 and 12 years, and 18 were 13 to 19 years. The vast majority of parents with children of this age, whether or not they lived with them, saw them every day or at least weekly. Only ten parents saw their children less often than this. Almost one in three members of the sample was also a grandparent. There were 70 men and 88 women within this category.

The adults in the survey gave the impression of considerable contact with children and young people. In addition to their role as parents, three quarters (373 of the total sample of 507) mentioned that they regularly spent time with children other than their own. Younger respondents, females, members of White majority ethnic groups, and those assigned the AB social grade, were most likely to have this additional contact. Mothers, whether working or not, typically fell within this category. When asked about the young people they had contact with, 233 of the 373 respondents mentioned family members (that is, other than their own children or grandchildren), 220 mentioned children of friends or neighbours, and 99 mentioned children they knew through work or voluntary work. The occupations of this latter group were, in order of frequency: 'other school worker', teacher;

general work (for example, in shop), out-of-school activities, childminder, nanny or other childcare provider, health professional such as doctor, dentist or nurse, social worker, local government or legal worker, and leisure centre worker.

Spending time together

Hardyment (1983) drew on child-rearing manuals and other evidence to trace the time parents and children have spent over recent centuries. Her interesting account, which says most about the lives of middle and upper class families, demonstrates that prior to 1820-70, children spent a large proportion of their time with adults. During the 18th century, most babies slept with their mothers or nurses and it was only in the 19th century that they were moved to their own rooms. Hardyment talks about 'mothers in command' during 1820-70. Fathers were becoming employed away from home, and their wives turned their energies to the home and children, taking responsibility for their children's health, moral well-being and education. Nursery staff were sometimes employed but rarely worked full time and did not play a dominant role in children's upbringing.

Changing social patterns beyond this date led to changes in routines. Women's social lives became much busier and they had less time to stay at home and look after children. Hardyment points out how women's magazines reflected the change in mood with fewer articles about motherhood, and many more about fashion, etiquette and the 'new woman'. Parents started to eat later in the evening and wanted more time on their own. As a result, children spent less and less time in their company. By the late 19th and the early 20th century, the nanny was at the peak of her influence. In the upper class families able to afford her services, many children spent most of their time in the nursery, seeing their parents only occasionally and at prescribed times. By the 1920s these nurses had become a social institution and were much depended on in many households. Hardyment writes how:

> More often than not, social commitments were still found to be inescapable − the fatal dinner party for which the Darlings left their children alone with the dog Nana was a symbol of a world from which children were excluded. In this uneasy period of adjustment, a wife's first duties were still towards her husband rather than her children.

More recent years have seen further changes in the day-to-day relationships between children and their parents and carers. While the paid nanny has all but disappeared, there has been the advent of the childminder and au pair as well as the widespread availability of nursery and other preschool places in which young children spend part or all of the day. Increased numbers of mothers going out to work, and accompanying shifts in lifestyle, have also had an impact. One change, as demonstrated by the National Family Mealtime Survey (Raisingkids, 2004), has been the demise of the communal evening meal that used to provide an opportunity for family members to get together. The passing of the familiar advertisement featuring the Oxo family at the dinner table can be seen as a symbol of this change.

All changes, however, have not been in a uniform direction and there are now many new opportunities these days for parents and children to do things together. Examples of a child-friendly society outlined elsewhere (see Chapter Eight) are illustrative.

The quality of relationships

Most evidence suggests that when they do things together, parents and their children tend to get on well. Relationships change as young people grow up but in many ways seem to improve. Gillies et al (2001) found that parents did not seem to find the teenage years particularly difficult and their 16- to 18-year-olds rejected the stereotype of teenagers growing away from their families. Indeed it emerged:

> ... how little the young people or their parents conformed to the stereotypes that are so often paraded about the teenage years.... Unlike Harry Enfield's comic creation, 'Kevin the teenager', many young people really do appreciate what their parents have to offer.

In another study (Langford et al, 2001), a 14-year-old said about parents:

> 'When you are younger you think it's like the thing you look up to.... But then as you get older, you find they are just human beings and they become more like really good friends....'

This study of 11- to 16-year-olds and their parents found that both generations valued their family life, and parents in particular viewed time spent together very positively. Girls especially valued the extra time they spent talking to their mothers as they grew older while boys were pleased that parental control had progressively got less.

Other authors have confirmed this encouraging picture of family life (Henricson, 2000; Cawson, 2002), which seems to be regarded particularly positively by girls and younger children. There are, nonetheless, other perspectives. One study, for instance, found that children reported how things can become more difficult between them and their parents when they get to about 13 years (NFPI, 2000).

It has been suggested that family relationships make a considerable difference to young people's confidence and self-esteem (Katz, 1997). Thirteen- and 19-year-old girls with confidence, optimism and motivation ('Can-do girls') were about twice as likely as others to say their parents talked to them and listened to their problems, and they were most likely to say they had loving parents, and could turn to their mothers for emotional support. A parallel study of boys found that a 'Can-do' attitude was linked to a positive parenting style which is emotionally supportive and involves listening to problems and views (Katz, 1999). It was also associated with families who did things together, and highly involved fathers who spent time with their sons and showed an interest in them.

The findings

These issues were pursued with children in the surveys who were asked two related questions on relationships between adults and children. First, did they think that adults enjoyed spending time with children and young people and, second, did they think that children and young people enjoyed spending time with adults?

More young people thought that adults liked doing things with them than thought they liked doing things with adults (Figure 7.1). Most acknowledged that both generations enjoy doing things together, but nonetheless recognised that there is no general rule.

Age affected views (Figures 7.2 and 7.3). As children got older they were less likely to think, first, that adults enjoyed being with children and young people and, second, that children and young people enjoyed being with adults. More than one in five in the oldest of the four age groups said that most people of their age do not really like spending time with adults. There was, however, somewhat of an imbalance as only one in ten of this age group thought that adults did not like doing things with them. Gender and ethnicity did not make a marked difference to responses.

Figure 7.1: Do adults enjoy spending time with children and young people, and vice versa? Responses of children (*n*=2,020)

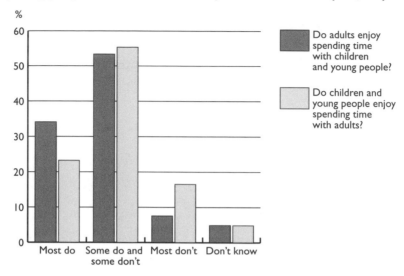

Figure 7.2: Do adults enjoy spending time with children and young people? Responses of children by age

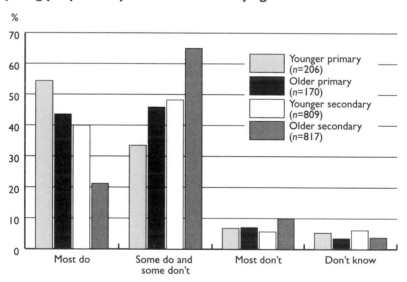

Do older and younger generations talk to each other?

Getting on together can mean listening and talking, and young people who described good relationships with their parents often mentioned

Figure 7.3: Do children and young people enjoy spending time with adults? Responses of children by age

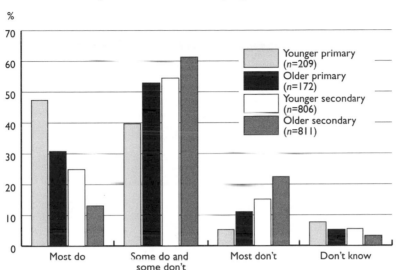

these activities. According to BT/ChildLine (2002), the things young people most want to talk about are bullying (mentioned by 65%), sex and relationships (58%), problems with school (53%), coping with a death in the family (44%), abuse (43%), and drugs (39%). Chapter Six reported how giving children and young people status and respect also involved letting them have a say in decisions that affected them.

To find out more about communication within the family, children were asked whether parents spent enough time talking to children and young people of their age, and whether children and young people spent enough time talking to adults.

It was interesting to find, in parallel with the findings on politeness and respect (see Chapter Six), that children in our survey were more likely to think that parents spent enough time talking to their children than children spent enough time talking to them (Figure 7.4). In other words, it was more common for young people to feel that 'most' adults spent enough time talking to young people than the reverse.

Age strongly affected these patterns (Figures 7.5 and 7.6). First, as young people got older they became less likely to think that children and young people talk to their parents enough. Of course it is difficult to know whether they think that they actually talk less or whether they talk to a similar extent but have a growing awareness of a need to talk more. There was a similar, although less marked, trend to suggest that as children grew older they were more likely to feel that parents do not talk to their children enough.

Figure 7.4: Do parents spend enough time talking to children and young people, and vice versa? Responses of children (n=2,017)

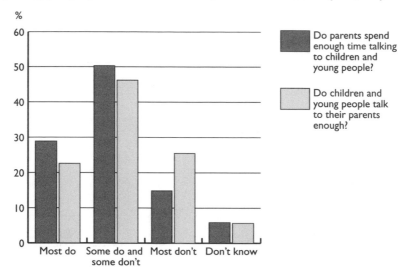

Figure 7.5: Do parents spend enough time talking to children and young people? Responses of children by age

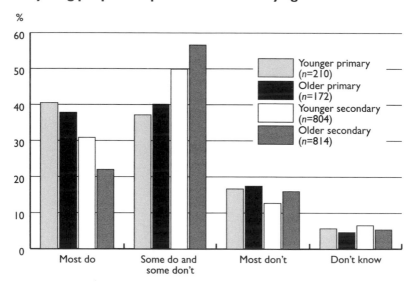

Gender also affected responses, although only as to whether children and young people spend enough time talking to parents. Boys were more likely than girls to think that most young people of their age do spend enough time, whereas girls were more likely to think that most do not. No differences emerged in relation to ethnicity.

Figure 7.6: Do children and young people talk to their parents enough? Responses of children by age

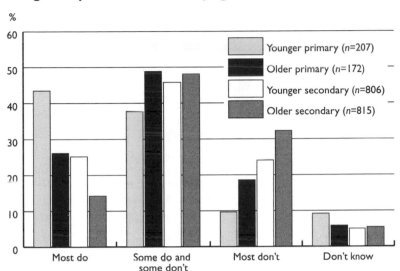

Adults were also asked for their views and whether or not they agreed with the statement 'Parents don't spend enough time talking with their teenagers'. Seven in ten adults agreed with this statement, and only 14% disagreed (Figure 7.7). Interestingly, they were divided on the question of whether things had changed since they were young. Whereas 41% thought parents talked less with their children nowadays, 34% thought they talked more, and 23% felt things were much the same as before.

Do older and younger generations listen to each other?

Similar questions were asked about whether young people and adults listen to each other, and broadly similar patterns were found (Figures 7.8, 7.9 and 7.10). First, there was a slight tendency for young people to be more likely to think that adults listen to them than that they listen to adults. Second, there were very strong effects of age with young people increasingly believing that neither adults nor young people listen to each other properly. Third, boys were more likely than girls to think that children do listen to adults properly. And fourth, there was no impact of ethnicity on responses to either question.

Figure 7.7: Adults' responses to the statement 'Parents don't spend enough time talking with their teenagers' (n=507)

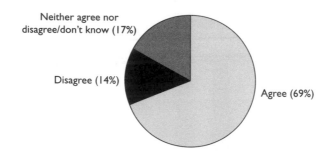

Neither agree nor disagree/don't know (17%)

Disagree (14%)

Agree (69%)

Figure 7.8: Do adults listen to children and young people properly, and vice versa? Responses of children (n=2,017)

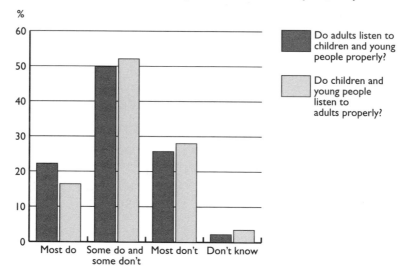

%

Do adults listen to children and young people properly?

Do children and young people listen to adults properly?

Most do   Some do and some don't   Most don't   Don't know

Adults' attitudes to their own and other people's children

Does having one's own children make a difference, and do adults regard their own children in a different light from children and young people in general? These questions were explored in the adult survey.

Three areas in particular were examined: whether children show respect towards adults, whether they lead carefree lives, and whether children make too many decisions for themselves. All adults were asked about their attitudes towards children in general, and parents of children between 6 and 19 years were also asked for their views in relation to their own children.

Figure 7.9: Do adults listen to children and young people properly? Responses of children by age

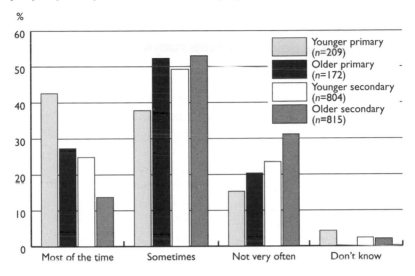

Figure 7.10: Do children and young people listen to adults properly? Responses of children by age

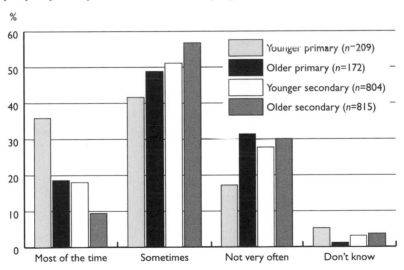

The 179 parents of children aged from 6 to 19 years did indeed see their own children in a special light. This was most striking for respect towards adults (Figure 7.11). Whereas only one in three parents agreed with the statement that 'Children and teenagers show enough respect for adults', nine in ten agreed that 'My children show enough respect towards adults'.

Although less marked, parents also made a clear distinction between decision making by children in general and by their own children (Figure 7.12). Overall, almost half the parents agreed that 'Young people make too many decisions for themselves' while only just over three in ten said 'My children make too many decisions for themselves'.

The picture was not much different for carefree lives (Figure 7.13). Whereas considerably less than half (44%) the parents said that 'Young people lead carefree lives', this proportion increased to six in ten for those saying 'My children lead carefree lives'.

It seems that parents tended to see their own children as more respectful to adults than most young people, and more likely to lead carefree lives, but less likely to have to make too many decisions for themselves. Parents appeared to regard themselves as good parents with positive attitudes towards their own children. At the same time, however, they held quite different attitudes towards children and young people more generally. Their constructions of childhood were quite distinct for children they knew and those they did not.

Figure 7.11: Parents' views on whether their own children, and young people in general, show enough respect for adults (n=179)

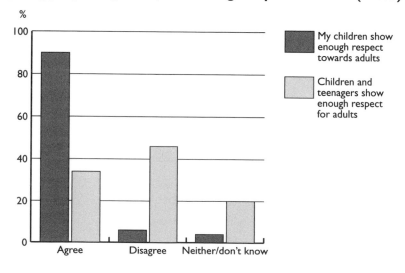

Figure 7.12: Parents' views on whether their children, and young people more generally, make too many decisions for themselves (n=179)

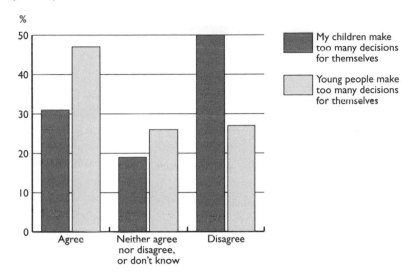

Figure 7.13: Parents' views on whether their own children, and young people in general, lead carefree lives (n=179)

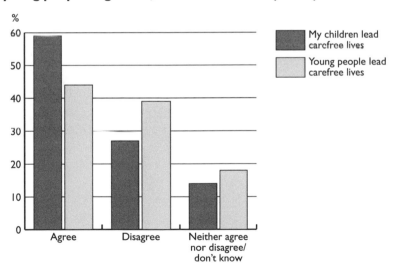

Summary

- Most adults, even if they were not parents, came into contact with children and young people in their daily lives.
- Children felt that adults are more likely to want to spend time with them than the other way around. As they grew older, they became less likely to think that the generations enjoy doing things together.
- Similarly, children were more likely to say that parents talk to their children enough than that children talk to their parents enough. Age again made a difference: older children were less likely than younger children to think that the generations talk to each other enough.
- Seven in ten adults agreed that parents do not spend enough time talking to their teenagers. Some thought parents talk to their children more nowadays than when they were young, and some thought the opposite is true.
- Similar patterns were found for children and adults listening to each other. Slightly more children overall said that adults listen to them than said they listen to adults, although patterns were strongly affected by age: increasingly, they felt that the generations did not listen to each other properly. Boys were more likely than girls to think that children listen to adults properly.
- There were striking differences in how adults regarded their own children and young people in general. For example, while nine in ten parents said their own children show enough respect towards adults, only one in three said the same for children and teenagers more generally.

"I think that teenagers are viewed badly in council estates and inner-city areas basically because they have nothing to do." (adult)

"Restaurants are not keen on children in this country. Bus drivers don't like pushchairs. Stately homes don't welcome children." (adult)

Adults could "respect children more (take away the 'only two schoolchildren at a time' signs in shops!). Listen to what children want (like letting children vote)." (female, Year 6)

"I think England is quite a good place to grow up in. But there are some bad things going on, like drugs." (male, Year 8)

"Most children are happy here and talk about England a lot." (female, Year 9)

"I'm sure you do hear about some of the good things [about children in the media] but they're not that big on page 26, and you don't remember stuff like that even if you read it." (adult)

'It doesn't matter where you go in the world, it's the same. People love their children." (adult)

EIGHT

A child-friendly society?

There is vociferous debate about whether or not England is a child-friendly country. On the one hand there is the clear view that we do not really like children all that much. The Mental Health Foundation (1999) writes:

> We claim to be a child-centred society, but in reality there is little evidence that we are. In many ways we are a ruthlessly adult-centred society where children are defined almost exclusively in terms of their impact on adult lives.... Our adult-centred society has tried to contain and limit the impact of children on adult life by either excluding them from much of it, blaming them for disturbing it or by admitting them only as designer accessories or treating them like pampered pets.

Hall (2003) discusses adolescence and quotes from Shakespeare's *The winter's tale* to make the point that things have changed little in this respect:

> I would there were no age between ten and three [thirteen] and twenty, or that youth would sleep out the rest; for there is nothing in the between but getting wenches with child, wronging the ancientry, stealing, fighting.

In Beresford's (2002) view, there is a broad "dislike of and discomfort with children in our society" that reflects adult ambiguity about children and inconsistent attitudes towards them. He points to how they are presented simultaneously as 'wayward' and 'innocent' and how, more than ever before, they are at once urged to grow up quickly but remain dependent.

On the other hand, however, Giddens (1998) writes how:

> We now live in the era of the 'prized child' ie the young person who gives fulfilment....

Many other very positive views on young people today attest to their achievements and the happiness they bring. In Lott's (2003) view, children's lives these days are rather better than the statistics suggest, and young people themselves have a lot going for them:

> They have been liberated from prejudice, are at the centre of family life, listened to, speak their own mind, and protected from cruelty. They are also recognised as consumers and portrayed as 'clever, powerful and knowing' by the advertising industry.

He concludes that children these days seem cheerful, "full of beans, of optimism, of creativity and curiosity" and that:

> ... if this generation is living through hell, then I can only say that it is a hell that the last generation could have only dreamed of.

Of course a wide range of attitudes towards children is only to be expected. Witness two letters alongside each other in a recent edition of the *Metro* (17 March 2003) about a case in which British Airways was criticised for the way it handled a distressed and screaming child. Whereas one took the view that:

> ... if their seats are paid for, kids are as entitled to mewl and puke as much as miserable old gits are to whinge and gripe

the other applauded the removal of the child from the flight and added:

> Perhaps this policy could be extended to include all forms of public transport, restaurants, pubs, cafes, cinemas, shops, supermarkets, parks, streets, government offices, theme parks, power stations, airports and bus shelters.

Changes in both directions

It is apparent that England has, in recent years, become more child friendly in some ways but less in others.

Children and childhood have in many senses achieved much greater status, and increasing legislation and advocacy for children's rights and participation in society have made a considerable difference. These include the overarching UN Convention on the Rights of the Child in 1989 (ratified by the UK government in 1991), the establishment of the first Minister for Children during 2003, the introduction of Children's Commissioners across the UK, and the new 2004 Children Act which it is hoped will radically change young people's services to maximise opportunity and minimise risk for every child and young person. The *Every child matters* Green Paper (DfES, 2003) identified five outcomes which matter most to children and young people: being healthy; staying safe; enjoying and achieving; making a positive contribution; and economic well-being.

Service developments run parallel. The *National service framework for children, young people and maternity services* (DH, 2003) recommends change in many areas including new standards to make hospitals more child friendly. Indeed these days most national initiatives and policies highlight the significance of young people's participation in the development and delivery of a wide range of provision. The government has taken this stance on board in directing all departments to provide greater opportunities for young people to become involved in the design, provision and evaluation of policies and services that affect them or which they use (CYPU, 2001).

In addition there are many relevant initiatives within the community, such as the Mayor of London's children and young people's strategy (GLA, 2004). This sets out a strategic framework to ensure children are given a voice and listened to, to develop a greater understanding of the diversity of London children's lives, and to provide improved services for children and young people in areas including health, education, safety and recreation.

The NSPCC Child Friendly Communities Programme is another example, as is the Kids in Museums campaign launched by *The Guardian* in response to a mother's letter about her young son who was asked to leave the Royal Academy for shouting. The manifesto for the campaign is based on readers' suggestions for making families welcome at galleries and museums and includes examples of places that have been recommended. Further examples are too numerous to mention.

Many would argue, nonetheless, that other forces in society are not so child friendly. It has already been shown how considerable child poverty remains, how demonisation of young people in the media continues, how young people feel they do not have enough to do, and how many feel worried about dangers that may face them in the community.

There is also concern that attitudes may be getting worse, or at least not any better. Evidence has been presented, for example, to suggest that many children feel excluded from decisions about, and use of, public spaces. Matthews and Limb (2000) explored the first of these issues with young people and found that most expressed a strong sense of disenfranchisement. Only one in four had ever talked to anyone (mainly friends, parents and relatives) about things they would like to see changed or added in their local area. Other studies have pointed to threats to safety in local parks (Franklin and Madge, 2000), how young people feel mistrusted and not respected by adults around them (Morrow, 2000), restricted in where they can go (O'Brien, 2000), under adult surveillance (Matthews et al, 2000), and commonly pushed aside by adults in shops (Brannen et al, 2000). Mayall (2002) concludes that:

> They feel that they are not accepted as rightful users of public space, that adults think they are in the wrong place at the wrong time, and that adults suspect their motives.

In many other areas, too, things may be less child friendly than in the past. Children and adults are more likely to lead separate lives as most mothers work and many young children 'grow up' in nurseries and education; maternal deprivation appears to have gone off the current agenda; and schools are increasingly preoccupied with the national curriculum and SATs, which reduces the emphasis on creative, artistic and recreational activities.

Are adults friendly and welcoming?

Children, young people and adults in the surveys were asked for their views on how friendly and welcoming England is to children and young people. Children were asked whether adults in England are friendly towards children (primary school level children) and young people (secondary school level children) of their age, and adults were asked to agree or disagree with the two statements that 'England is a country that is friendly towards children' and 'England is a country that is friendly towards teenagers'.

It is worth noting that only a minority was prepared to say that most adults are friendly towards them, and that this proportion dropped with age (Figure 8.1). So while 30% of the younger primary school children did regard adults as generally friendly, only about half as many of the older secondary school children were in agreement. This does not mean they thought adults were unfriendly, but it suggests most of them recognise that adults were individuals and that while some were friendly, others were not.

Figure 8.1: Are adults in England friendly towards children and young people? Responses of children by age

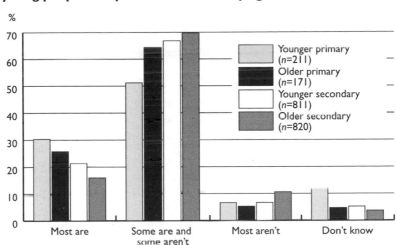

Ethnicity affected responses at primary but not at secondary school level, and almost twice as many 'White' as 'Other ethnicity' children of this age (32% as against 17%) said that most adults are friendly to children like them.

Children's constructions of childhood show similarities with adults' constructions in suggesting that grown-ups have rather different views of children and teenagers and regard the former more positively. As Figure 8.2 shows, adults were considerably more likely to agree that England is friendly towards children than towards teenagers. In fact,

Figure 8.2: Is England friendly towards children and teenagers? Responses of adults (*n*=507)

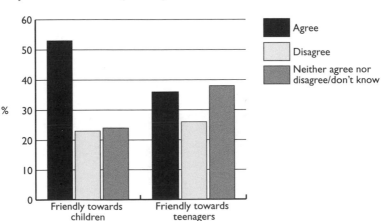

over half the sample (53%) agreed with the first statement but only just over one in three (36%) agreed with the second. Rather more adults were unsure what they thought about public attitudes to teenagers than were unclear about attitudes towards younger children.

Are children made welcome in public places?

Children were also asked whether they were made to feel welcome in public places such as shops, restaurants and leisure centres. Well over half said that they were most of the time. Most of the rest indicated that they felt welcome sometimes, but one in ten said they did not very often feel welcome (Figure 8.3).

Gender and age did not make a big difference to these patterns. Ethnicity, however, seemed to have more impact. As shown in Figure 8.4, 53% of 'White' children, but 43% of 'Other ethnicity' children, said they feel welcome in these public places. Within ethnicity groups, gender seemed to make a further difference. Males said much the same whatever their ethnicity, but 'White' females showed some tendency to feel more welcome in public places than females in the 'Other ethnicity' group.

And what did the adults say? Asked whether children were made to feel welcome in public places, just under half said they were while one in three said they were not.

Figure 8.3: Do you feel welcome in places like shops, restaurants and leisure centres? Responses of children by age

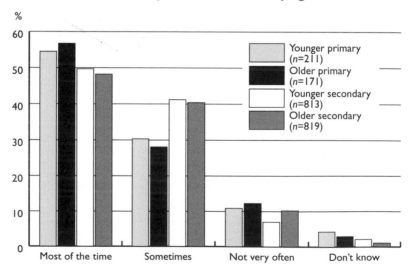

Figure 8.4: Do you feel welcome when you go to places like shops, restaurants and leisure centres? Responses of secondary school children by ethnicity

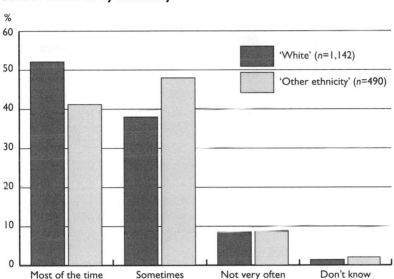

Children in neighbourhoods

Another index of a child-friendly country is the degree to which adults are happy to see children and young people in and around the neighbourhood playing and doing other things that they enjoy. Children and adults were asked whether they think adults in England like seeing children play. Except for the very youngest children, they were most likely of all to say that some adults enjoy seeing children playing in their neighbourhood but that others do not (Figure 8.5). Again, young people become less likely to see adults as definitely welcoming as they get older. Neither gender nor ethnicity seemed to make a difference to these patterns.

Adults took a somewhat different stance. They were considerably more positive than the young people when asked to agree or disagree with the statement 'I enjoy seeing children playing in my neighbourhood'. If their views are representative of all adults, it is encouraging to find that over three in four say they do enjoy seeing children playing in their neighbourhood and fewer than one in ten indicate they do not. Parents are more likely than non-parents to say they welcome children playing in their neighbourhood.

We also asked adults about their attitudes towards teenagers. Did

Figure 8.5: Do adults enjoy seeing children playing in their neighbourhood? Responses of children by age

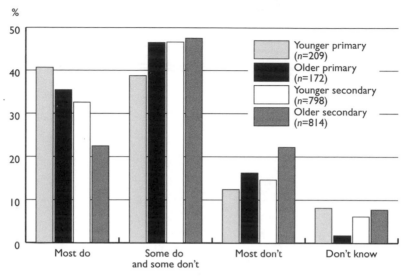

they agree or disagree with the statement 'I feel threatened by groups of teenagers hanging around in streets and public places'? Over half said they do feel threatened (Figure 8.6), and these were particularly likely to be women, older respondents, and those with no regular contact with young people. This confirms the findings of other investigations (for example, Measor and Squires, 2000) that have pointed out how adults can feel uncomfortable when confronted by gatherings of young people in the community.

Figure 8.6: Adults' responses to the statement 'I feel threatened by groups of teenagers hanging around in streets and public places' (n=507)

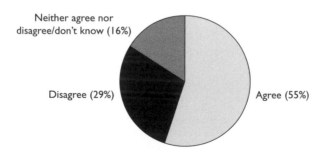

Growing up in England

It has already been shown that adults see England as a country more friendly towards children than teenagers. To find out whether children agree with this, they were asked if they thought England is a good country for a child or young person to grow up in.

Primary school level children were more likely than children at secondary school level to say that England is child friendly (Figure 8.7), a finding that mirrored what the adults said. Most, whatever their age, were more likely to say that it is *quite* good rather than *very* good, partly because they recognised things they liked as well as things they disliked. Asked to explain their responses in their own words, 361 of the 383 primary school children, and 1,400 of the 1,657 at secondary level, commented on the things they do and do not like about England.

Five main reasons why England is a good place to live stood out for primary school children: it meets most needs, it provides good education and other services, is generally safe, has people who are kind and friendly, and gives plenty of opportunities for things to do. The things they did not like were mainly to do with the environment and included crime, vandalism, danger and dirt. They also mentioned the war in Iraq (in progress at the time of the survey).

For the secondary school children, the most important positive aspects seemed to be good education and other services followed, in order, by safety, jobs and equal opportunities, things to do and places

Figure 8.7: Is England a good country to grow up in? Responses of children by age

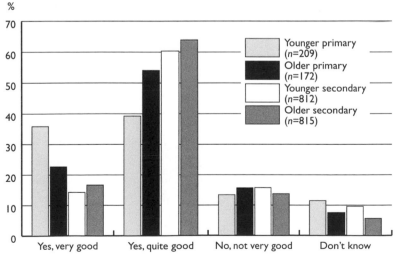

to go, friendly people, and good provision that meets needs. More negatively, they pointed to dangers in the environment and, in the case of a small band of young people, the shortage of things to do that are free. Again there were some with mixed views who liked some things but not others. A few children were not sure what they felt as they had lived in England all their lives and perhaps had not thought about this question before. Another 15 said, quite simply, that their country was better than others. The comments children made are illustrated further below.

Meeting needs

At least 44 primary school children explained how England is rich and meets most needs. Many of these specifically mentioned healthy food and water and the fact that there is plenty to eat. A further 58 children at secondary school level described England as a rich country that provides the necessary things and has a good supply of healthy food and water.

"We have most things we need."

Education and other services

Good free education was mentioned by 28 primary school children. An additional 15 noted how there are other good services (including emergency services) to help people. Young people at secondary school level agreed and a total of 138 pointed to the good education they receive in England. Another 75 mentioned good services and laws:

"There are lots of services to help people."

A safe country?

Primary school children were uncertain how safe it was to live in England. On the one hand, 20 said England was a safe country and a nice place to live. These added that children were not in danger and the country was free from terrorism or war. On the other hand, some pointed out that certain localities could be very dangerous. Over 30 children referred to crime, violence and kidnappings, and a further 19 listed 'war in Iraq' as negative factors influencing life in England.

Secondary school children were also concerned with safety. A total of 127 thought England was safe or quite safe, and some of these pointed to the lack of natural disasters and the absence of terrorism and war.

Kind and friendly people

There were some differences of opinion about the characteristics of people living in England. A total of 24 primary school children thought that kind, friendly and nice people made England a good place to live. Another six referred positively to friends and other children. Thirteen, however, suggested that while some people were nice, others were nasty. Nine mentioned 'weird', 'bad' or 'aggressive' people as a reason for saying England was not a nice place to live.

At secondary school level, 80 children said they thought England was a friendly place and that they liked their friends and other children. Five, however, suggested that England did not like children very much. Fourteen stressed the positive value of a multicultural society while five pointed to the negative aspect of racism:

"Some people feel welcome and some don't."

Plenty to do

The availability of clubs, facilities, entertainment and fun places to go was why 18 primary school children liked living in England. Two others simply said that it was fun being in the country and it made them happy. Having things to do and places to go was important to young people, and 95 secondary school children specifically said there were good opportunities of this kind in England. On the other hand, however, 20 young people noted how there were not many things to do that were free:

"It can get boring."

The environment

Apart from dangers in the environment, a few primary school children pointed to the rubbish and mess in their locality as well as vandalism and drugs. Two said that only bad things happen. A considerable number of secondary school children also mentioned dangerous and unpleasant aspects of the environment in England, and 201 listed things they did not like. Crime, violence, murder and kidnap were mentioned by 76, and 'druggies', child offenders and 'weird' people by another 61. Unspecified dangers were cited by 15, and eight mentioned the consequences of war in Iraq. A further 41 talked about rubbish, bad smells and pollution as among the things contributing to a poor environment.

Jobs and opportunities

It is clear that, with age, opportunities for work become more important. It was not surprising that the chances of employment were mentioned positively by 107 secondary school pupils:

> "People give other people chances."

In general

Many young people, whatever their age, mentioned both positive and negative aspects of growing up in England. Some of their comments were:

> "There's a lot of houses and quiet areas but there's also a lot of litter and pollution."
>
> "There's some places are safe but some aren't."
>
> "It's okay, but at the moment everywhere is a bad place to live."
>
> "I would rather live in Spain."

Adults' views on whether England is child friendly

To explore adults' attitudes to England as a child-friendly country, they were asked to compare it with other countries and say whether it was a lot or a little more child friendly, the same, or a little or a lot less child friendly. Views were mixed (Figure 8.8). Overall, just over a quarter said it was a lot or a little more child friendly, a further quarter said it was the same, and the remaining just under a half said it was a little or a lot less child friendly.

Figure 8.8: How child friendly are we compared to other countries? Responses of adults (*n*=507)

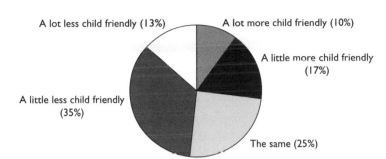

A lot less child friendly (13%)

A lot more child friendly (10%)

A little more child friendly (17%)

A little less child friendly (35%)

The same (25%)

Women were less likely than men to think England was child friendly. More (49% compared to 37%) said it was a lot or a little less child friendly than other countries, and this was the view of 55% of mothers with children up to 19 years.

Adults were given the opportunity to explain in their own words why they thought that England was more or less child friendly than other countries. The reasons they gave are shown in Figures 8.9 and 8.10. Those who said it was more child friendly were most likely to point to the abuse of children abroad.

"You've only got to watch the TV and read the newspapers to see the poor and neglected children in other countries. You don't see many children in this country starving ... . It's a democratic country."

Figure 8.9: Why is England more child friendly? Responses of adults who stated 'England is a little or a lot more child friendly' (*n*=123)

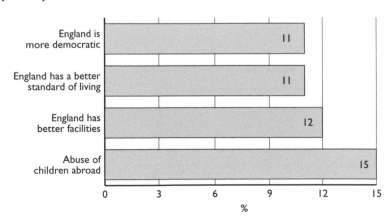

England is more democratic — 11

England has a better standard of living — 11

England has better facilities — 12

Abuse of children abroad — 15

%

Figure 8.10: Why is England less child friendly? Responses of adults who stated 'England is a little or a lot less child friendly' (*n*=219)

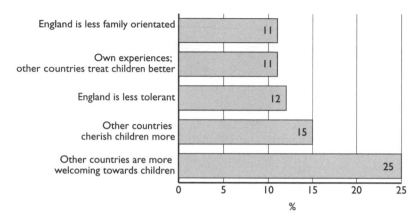

Three other reasons also stood out. These were that England had better facilities than other countries, a better standard of living, and that it was more democratic:

> "We are a country which provides one of the best welfare services in the world and there are many things geared towards children."
>
> "I have noticed we are more careful with protecting children in public places."
>
> "We acknowledge their rights more. We do acknowledge them as young people and see them as our future."
>
> "We are more liberal."

Adults also had views on why England was less child friendly than other countries, and their reasons fell into five broad, although overlapping, categories. The most common was that other countries were more welcoming towards children:

> "You are more welcome in more places with your children (in other countries). You see more people out with their children. Here, children seem to be excluded from family occasions."
>
> "When you go abroad, they are more welcome in places than they are over here."

Linked to this, adults said they thought children were loved and cherished more in other places:

"They love kids abroad and make a fuss and treasure them."

Another common view was that other countries were more tolerant towards young people:

"They are more tolerant and put their children first and are more protective."

"Attitudes to young people in public seem to be more relaxed in Europe."

Furthermore, in their own experience, children seemed to be treated better in other countries where the culture was more family orientated:

"We could probably do a lot more for our children and teenagers. We do not include them enough in family gatherings and get-togethers. We are not allowed to take them into (pubs and clubs) unless they are a certain age. We could do more in that respect. Abroad, children are involved in every part of family life, and their needs and requests are taken into consideration. We do not do that, we are more stand-offish. We tend to be backward in coming forward where our children are concerned. We do not talk to them enough."

"My own children embarrass me in this country but not abroad."

"I think having visited other countries, that children are more welcomed in other places. I think generally there is a more liberal attitude toward children and that in turn sort of creates a sense of responsibility in children themselves."

"I think we think that children are trouble and go against all our rules. Abroad they tend to be more loved and adored and cherished."

Many adults, however, did not see England as more or less child friendly than other countries and felt that things were much the same wherever you go:

"From my experience, it is not any different to other parts of the world."

"Everywhere I've been, everyone likes children."

"Different cultures have their own values and different ways of dealing with children."

"I have found that if children are well behaved, they are acceptable in any country."

"I haven't noticed anything different. The pressures are the same. Kids are kids."

In particular, it depends on the countries England is being compared with:

"Some countries really abuse their children through slave labour and cheap labour, yet other countries like Spain look after their kids better than us."

"Some countries use child labour, but some developed countries are more tolerant to children. We are in the middle."

There was also an acknowledgement that things are changing:

"Children are allowed to go into places that they weren't before. Not many places exclude children. It is nice to see young people."

"The education system is better and has improved. We do have theme parks where you can take your children. The leisure industry is geared more towards children than it used to be."

Finally, some adults pointed out that there is more than one way of looking at most things:

"Because I haven't had evidence around me that tells me any different. I think a lot of it is received wisdom. You're told that the Italians absolutely love their babies, but I can't say that they love their kids anymore than my daughter-in-law loves her children. They certainly dress them up more flamboyantly in Italy, but that is not necessarily a sign that they are more geared towards children. They're just showing off their children more."

"Your attitudes are going to be different for two weeks while you're away as well. So it's going to be seen through those rose tinted glasses."

"We love our children but we don't take them out to play as much as other countries do. In some European countries, they eat out altogether when the kids are quite young. We don't do that."

Young people's portrayal in the media

How the media portrays young people publicly is a reflection of child friendliness. Adults were asked what they thought about media representations of children and were presented with nine possible descriptions of their portrayal. Three of these were essentially negative ('as troublemakers', 'negatively' and 'as victims'), three were generally positive ('as an asset to the community', 'positively' and 'respectfully'), two indicated something about the presentation of childhood ('as mini adults' and 'as innocents'), and one was indeterminate ('accurately'). The adults were asked to select all correct descriptions (Figure 8.11).

The adults very clearly felt that much media coverage of young people is negative. Three quarters of the sample selected 'as troublemakers'. This was followed by 'negatively' (47%) and 'as mini adults' (also 47%). The most positive options of 'as an asset to the community', 'positively' and 'accurately' were mentioned far less often (by only 13%, 11% and 9% of the sample respectively).

During the course of interviews, adults mentioned some of the ways in which they thought the media had an impact on relationships

Figure 8.11: How adults saw young people portrayed in the media (n=507)

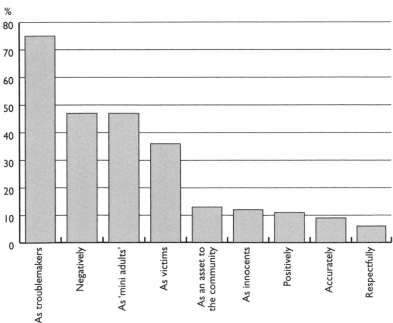

between adults and young people, and on perceptions of children in society. The following comments are illustrative:

> "Because of the media putting about such things as paedophilia it has frightened people and put people off doing things with children."
>
> "Because there's a media presumption that your children are going to behave badly the moment they walk through the door. Almost like people are waiting for them to be naughty. This is what I feel when we're out. I don't like taking them out to restaurants, places where they have to sit for long times and behave."

It was apparent that the adults saw the media as publicising negative constructions of childhood.

Do adults really prefer their pets?

It is commonly claimed that 'Englishmen prefer their pets', and generally their dogs, to their children. We could not resist asking adults in the survey for their views on this matter.

The source of this claim is elusive. However, much of the argument seems to revolve around the comparative history, status and wealth of two main organisations in the area, the National Society for the Prevention of Cruelty to Children (NSPCC) and the Royal Society for the Prevention of Cruelty to Animals (RSPCA).

It is certainly true that the RSPCA came into earlier being, and it seemed that in part this reflected the activities of Dick Martin, commonly known as 'Humanity Dick', who introduced the first bill offering protection to domestic animals to the House of Commons around 1822. It was probably also partly because parental rights were considered paramount. It appears that while Lord Shaftesbury, a famous reformer, agreed in around 1881 that many children were suffering cruelty and neglect, he also advanced the argument that looking after children was a private matter and not something to be addressed by legislation. The NSPCC came into existence in 1884, and it is apparent that its development was closely linked to the establishment of the RSPCA.

There are various versions as to what exactly happened. One is that, following the establishment of the SPCA (the American counterpart of the RSPCA) in New York, a woman on her death-bed made a dying wish to help a child, living in the next room with her mother, who was left alone all day without food and beaten severely every night. The charitable worker charged with the message received no support from the police or her lawyer who said it was not possible to intervene between parents and children. Undaunted, she went to the co-founder of the SPCA and told of a little animal that was being badly treated. After he promised to help, she revealed that the little animal was in fact a child. He investigated the matter and brought the case to court, contending that the child was an animal. The case was won. As a result, a great many other cases of child cruelty came to light which led to the founding of a New York Society for the Prevention of Cruelty to Children. The Society for the Prevention of Cruelty to Children in England was established shortly afterwards, and the help of the RSPCA in forming this sister organisation was publicly acknowledged. The co-founder of the New York SPCA became a member of the NSPCC Council and Committee and established a strong link between the societies promoting child and animal welfare.

Certainly links between child abuse and animal abuse have been acknowledged for centuries. Becker (2001) notes how the philosopher John Locke wrote about the association, the artist William Hogarth condemned cruelty to animals and pointed to the consequences for humans, and the anthropologist Margaret Mead suggested that children who are cruel to animals may become anti-social and violent in later life. Recent research, some in the UK but mainly in the US, has lent some support to these ideas (Becker and French, 2004).

It is often asked why there is a royal society for animals but 'only' a national society for children, and the reasons are again largely historic. The NSPCC, which began life as the London Society for the Prevention of Cruelty to Children, was in fact granted a Royal Charter of Incorporation by Queen Victoria in 1895 and she became Royal Patron some years later. In more recent times, Princess Elizabeth was President between 1944 and 1952, followed by her sister Princess Margaret. As far as the RSPCA is concerned, the 'Royal' prefix was also due to the patronage of Queen Victoria, who offered support and encouragement to the society's activities throughout her reign.

The findings

To find out what adults in the survey thought about attitudes to children and pets, they were asked to indicate whether they agreed, disagreed, or neither agreed nor disagreed with the statement 'The English love their dogs more than their children'. As shown below (Figure 8.12), they were very divided in their views. Overall, one in three agreed

Figure 8.12: Adults' responses to the statement 'The English love their dogs more than their children' (*n*=507)

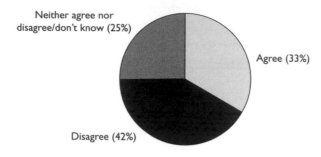

Neither agree nor
disagree/don't know (25%)

Agree (33%)

Disagree (42%)

with the statement, four in ten disagreed, and one in four were not sure. Females (36% compared with 30% of males), older age groups (39% of those over 55 years, but 29% of those between 20 and 44), and non-parents (37% as contrasted with 30% of parents), were most likely to agree.

Summary

- Only a minority of young people were prepared to say that most adults are friendly towards them, and this proportion dropped with age. The predominant view was that some adults are friendly but others are not.
- At primary level, almost twice as many 'White' children as children from 'Other ethnicity' backgrounds said most adults are friendly to children of their age.
- Adults were much more likely to say that England is friendly towards children than towards teenagers.
- Over half the young people said they usually felt welcome in public places such as shops, restaurants and leisure centres. Children from 'Other ethnicity' backgrounds were least likely to take this view.
- Just under half the adults agreed that children are made to feel welcome in public places. One in three thought they are not.
- Adults were more likely than young people to say that adults like to see children playing in their neighbourhoods.
- Over half the adults said they sometimes feel threatened by groups of teenagers hanging around in streets and public places. These were particularly likely to be women, older people, and those who had little contact with young people.

- As children got older they were less likely to regard England as a good country to grow up in. Most, whatever their age, did, however, point to aspects they like as well as those they dislike.
- Half the adults thought that England is a little or a lot less child friendly than other countries, while just over a quarter said it is a lot or a little more child friendly.
- Adults gave a very clear indication that they regard media coverage of young people as predominantly negative.
- Adults were divided on the question of whether the English love their dogs more than their children. One in three thought they do while one in four said they do not.

"I think it comes down to the Victorian attitude that children should be seen and not heard. It's slowly turning round. I think people need to change their attitudes. The responsibility is ultimately with the parents to change their attitudes and other people will follow." (adult)

"I think I could make adults happier by being kind and helpful and polite." (female, Year 3)

"One thing adults could do is pay just a bit more attention. One other thing is to be a bit more encouraging." (male, Year 4)

"There need to be more opportunities for younger people." (female, Year 9)

"Healthcare for children in this country is second to none." (adult)

NINE

Making things better for children and adults

The findings from earlier chapters suggest that there are many ways in which young lives could be improved. The role of government and other agencies in meeting young people's needs more effectively, encouraging their greater participation in decisions that affect them, and generally making England more child friendly, have been touched upon, as have young people's concerns about safety, leisure activities, the environment and a host of other areas in their daily lives. This chapter focuses on what children and adults in the surveys said about things they would like to see done in the community as well as how people could make each other's lives happier and more enjoyable in everyday ways. They were asked, for instance, to suggest what adults could do for young people of their age, and what they might do to make life easier and happier for adults.

Hallett and Prout (2003) discuss how children's voices can influence social policy, and several exercises other than the present study have sought to find out children's priorities were they in a position of power. The Children's and Young People's Unit (see Flood, 2002) received back completed postcards from over 700 children aged 12 or less saying what they would change for children if they were Prime Minister. Their responses were coded into six categories, and much the most important was 'achievement and enjoyment' (mentioned by 483 children and including actions to do with school, the environment and leisure). Protection (104 mentions) came next, followed by health and well-being (73), participation and citizenship (47), inclusion (30), and responsibility (21). Sinclair et al (2002) report the findings of a similar survey based on young people's messages on postcards about what they would do to make things better for young people if they were Tony Blair. The best information was collected from 12- to 14-year-olds whose priorities were, in order of importance: better services for young people; better facilities and activities; involvement in charity/helping others; better safety for children; children's participation; learning about others; more freedom; and improving the environment.

The school survey and young people's concerns

The present study also gave all children the opportunity to imagine they were Prime Minister and say what they would do for children and young people of their age. Five possibilities were suggested for them to choose from. The questions were worded slightly differently for the primary and secondary school children although the meaning in each case was broadly similar. At primary school level the choice was between: making sure children were safe; making sure children felt cared for; making sure there was always someone there to help children; making sure all children had enough money, food and clothes; and making sure children could say what they thought. For the older group the options were: making sure young people were safe; making young people feel valued; providing good services for young people and their families if they needed them; ensuring a good standard of living for all young people; and making sure young people had opportunities to say what they thought.

'Ensuring safety' emerged as the clear priority for the number one thing young people would do if they were Prime Minister (Figure 9.1). Around half those in each age grouping ranked this first, and this rose to over six in ten among the younger secondary school children. 'A good standard of living' was a second main priority, followed by one of the other options depending upon age.

Figure 9.1: If you were Prime Minister: number one priorities for services. Responses of children by age

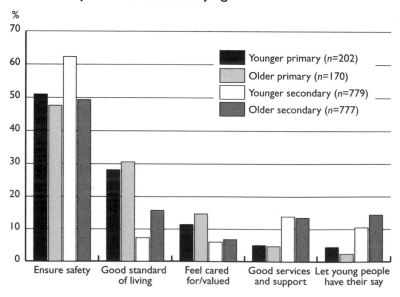

Choices were also ranked and all responses taken into account in a second examination of priorities (Figure 9.2). Looking at mean ranks instead of number one priorities provides a slightly different picture. In this instance, 'ensuring safety' remains top of the list but 'a good standard of living' stands out less. Age seems to make a difference to views with 'feeling cared for and valued' becoming less significant with age but 'letting young people have their say' becoming more important.

Figure 9.2: If you were Prime Minister. Mean ranks of children by age (higher ranks assume greater importance)

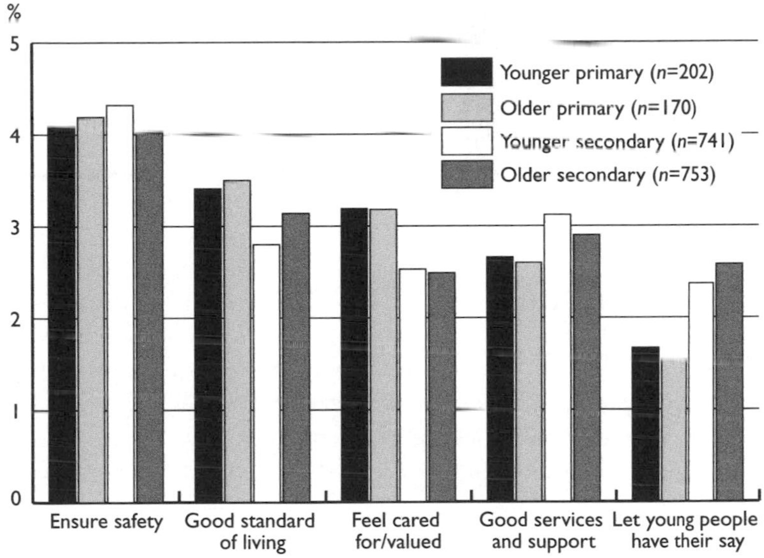

Young people and their leisure activities

Young people had an opportunity to say what they thought about leisure activities available to them. Asked if they had enough things to do when out of school, over half the sample said that they did most of the time (Figure 9.3). A further quarter, however, and a proportion steeply rising with age, indicated that this was true only sometimes. At least another one in ten said they rarely had enough to do. These findings bear out the much-vaunted claim that what many young people want more than anything else are more leisure and sporting activities. Looking at patterns within the sample, it seemed that girls and children from 'Other ethnicity' backgrounds were more likely than boys and children describing themselves as 'White' to be dissatisfied in this respect.

Figure 9.3: Do you have enough things to do? Responses of children by age

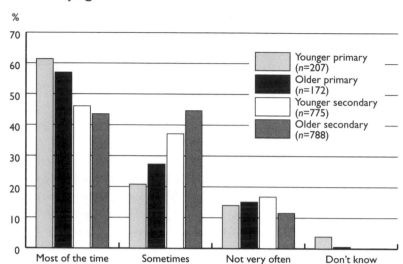

Adults' priorities

Adults were asked to indicate their own priorities for promoting a child-friendly society. What they said closely mirrored the responses of the young people in seeing protection as most important, and encouraging young people to express their views as least important (Figure 9.4).

Adults were also asked if they agreed with three statements: 'There aren't enough sources of help and advice for children and teenagers'; 'Sufficient priority is given to ensuring the physical safety of young people'; and 'Children and teenagers are provided with enough opportunities for leisure activities'. Their responses are shown below (Table 9.1).

Parents and grandparents were more likely than non-parents to think there was a shortage of help and advice for young people, as were non-working compared with working mothers. There was more agreement on whether sufficient priority was given to ensuring the physical safety of young people, although there was a tendency for women, older respondents and parents to show most concern. Older age groups and non-parents were most likely to think that children and teenagers had enough things to do in their leisure time.

Figure 9.4: Adults' number one priorities for promoting a child-friendly society (n=507)

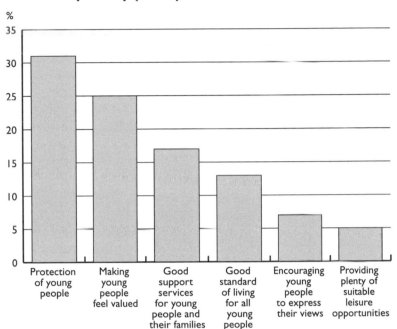

Table 9.1: Adults' views on provision and support for young people

	Agree (%)	Neither/ don't know (%)	Disagree (%)
There aren't enough sources of help and advice for children and teenagers	55	21	24
Sufficient priority is given to ensuring the physical safety of young people	44	19	37
Children and teenagers are provided with enough opportunities for leisure activities	39	11	50

Making lives easier and happier

Daily lives can be improved not only through changes to social policies and services, but also by everyday actions at a personal level. To encourage children to think about what could be done in these ways, they were asked what they thought adults, children and young people could do to make things easier and more enjoyable for each other. Questions on how they could improve adults' lives were included in recognition of the moral competencies of children that are present from a young age (Mayall, 2002). As they grow older and more experienced, these become more marked and children are able to demonstrate strong commitments to members of their families as well as concern for their welfare.

What adults could do for children and young people

At the end of the survey questionnaire, primary school children were asked to suggest two things adults could do to make children happier, and children at secondary school were asked to suggest two things adults could do to make life easier and more enjoyable for children and young people. At primary level, 364 children made at least one suggestion and 215 of these made a second suggestion too, and at secondary level the numbers making one suggestion, and two suggestions, were 1,220 and 597 respectively.

Responses were grouped into seven main categories: spoil them more; improve the local/world environment; talk more/listen more/spend more time together; treat young people better; fewer restrictions; expect less from young people; and provide more things to do. An 'other' category was included for responses that did not fit within any of these. The following figure (Figure 9.5) shows the proportions of primary and secondary school level children who gave responses falling within one of these broad categories.

At primary school level, the most common suggestion was that adults could talk and listen more to children, and spend more time with them. This was followed closely by spoiling them more. Treating young people better, providing them with more things to do, and imposing fewer restrictions were next in order of importance. Similar patterns emerged at secondary school level, although the extent to which priorities were mentioned varied. For these older children, being treated better came top, followed closely by talking and listening more and spending more time with young people. Fewer restrictions, more things to do, and being spoiled more, came next.

Some gender differences were found. At primary school level, the main difference between boys and girls was that males were more likely to say that adults should spoil them more. To a lesser extent, girls showed a greater wish for adults to talk, listen and spend more time with them, and treat them better. For secondary school children, too, there was a tendency for boys to say they would like to be spoiled more while girls wanted adults to spend time with them, talking and listening, and make them feel happier and more valued.

Figure 9.5: What adults could do to improve the lives of children and young people. Responses of children by age

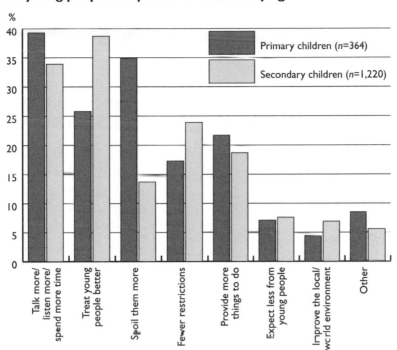

The talking/listening/spending more time category also covered adults paying young people more attention, providing more support, showing more interest, offering advice, helping with homework, and encouraging children to talk and say what they thought. Having fun and playing with children were, in addition, mentioned as important.

Treating young people better meant, for many, making them feel valued and happier. It was suggested that adults could love their children more, hug them, be kind, friendly and nice, praise them more, make them feel wanted and important, and trust them more. They could also be less strict, shout and tell off less, and take young people more seriously. There was a plea to treat children the same as they treated each other, and not to treat young people as if they were all troublemakers or babies. "Let children be themselves", "accept that they are growing up", and "give them a chance", were some of the comments.

Younger children were particularly likely to say that adults could spoil them more, and what they had in mind was buying them more things, giving them more money and treats, and doing more for them. "Give us all the sweets in the world", "drive children everywhere they want to go", and "tidy our rooms" were some of the specific things they said.

Those wanting fewer restrictions mentioned being able to go out more, go to bed when they liked, stay out later, have friends over, do more "stuff", and have more freedom. Some said they wanted more choice and responsibility, and they did not want adults to comment on their clothes and hair. They thought young people should be allowed to have friends of any culture, watch their favourite television programmes without interruption, and play computer and playstation games all the time.

Calls for more things to do focused on a greater range of after-school activities, youth clubs, parks, facilities and shops for children. Some said young people should be taken out more and given the chance to go to new places. One suggestion was that there should be pubs for kids!

Making the environment, country or world a better place to live in was not a major priority for young people. However, making parks and environments safer and less polluted, and ensuring no wars, litter, child abuse, violence or murders, were noted by some. More facilities for needy people, fewer laws and rules, an end to racism, and a ban on cigarettes, drugs and alcohol, were also mentioned. Different views on the police were put forward: on the one hand, the police should not be so strict but, on the other, there should be more policing as young people get away with too much.

Not many young people said that adults should expect less from them, but those who did mentioned not having to do washing-up and housework, and giving children the opportunity to do nothing and relax. "Give us more free time", "put less pressure on us", "stop nagging" and "leave us alone", they said. Less responsibility, more time off school, no homework, and not so many tests at school, were some other suggestions.

What children and young people could do for adults

The reciprocal questions were also posed. Primary school children were asked to write down two things children could do to make adults happier, and secondary school children were asked to suggest two things children and young people could do to make life easier and more enjoyable for adults. In all, 366 children at primary level made one suggestion and 257 made two. At secondary level, 1,139 children made one suggestion and 639 made two.

Responses were again grouped into categories and comparisons drawn between different age groups. The seven main categories of response were: talk to/listen to/spend more time; be nicer; do things for them; be responsible and mature; behave better; give them space; and make them proud of you (Figure 9.6).

Over half the primary school children thought that young people their age could behave better, and almost four in ten said they could be nicer. The only other things mentioned by more than one in ten were doing things for adults, talking and listening to them more, and spending more time with them. Secondary school children were most likely to say that young people could be nicer to adults (over half suggested this), and around one in four said they could spend more time with them, behave better, and be responsible and mature.

Although there were few gender differences at primary school level, girls were more likely to stress being nicer to adults and doing things for them while boys tended to emphasise the need to be more responsible and mature. At secondary level, girls thought young people could talk and listen to adults more, spend more time with them and be nicer, while boys were again more likely to stress the need to be more responsible and mature.

Being nicer (and more considerate) was described as treating adults with respect, not hurting their feelings, treating them as young people

Figure 9.6: What children and young people could do to improve the lives of adults. Responses of children by age

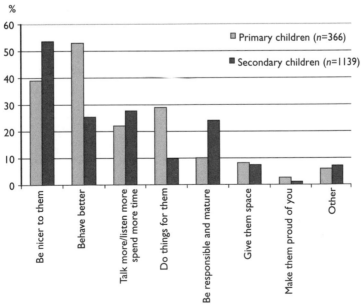

would like to be treated themselves, not making them angry or upset, not being nasty or cheeky, and not getting them 'stressed out'. The aim should be to make adults happy, make them feel like a parent, understand their point of view, not think parents are an embarrassment, and tell them you love them. Being nicer also meant not being greedy, selfish, noisy, moody, sulky or grumpy. Smile, be happy, calm down, relax, don't fight with brothers and sisters, and don't lie or bully, were some of the things the young people thought they could do to improve adults' lives.

A few mentioned specific things young people could do for adults. Among their suggestions were looking after them, hugging them, cooking them dinner, giving them breakfast in bed, and teaching them to play playstation.

Some of the suggestions for being responsible and mature were about not staying out too late and keeping in touch by mobile phone, not asking for too much money, not running into roads, shoplifting or doing anything illegal, getting into drugs or smoking, dropping litter, making a mess, or breaking rules. Some felt that young people could do more for themselves, take punishments, and even raise money for disabled people.

In addition, some young people said that they should let adults have their own space, allow them more time to themselves, let them have an easy life, let them spend time together, give them peace and quiet, stop annoying and nagging them. Finally, there were a few who suggested they could do things to make adults proud of them. These included working hard, doing well at home and school, and just doing "good things".

Summary

- Whatever their age, young people felt that ensuring their safety is a number one priority. This is more important to them than a good standard of living, feeling cared for and valued, good services and support, or letting young people have their say.
- Adults also saw child protection as a key issue for policy and practice.
- Over half the adults felt there are not enough sources of help and advice for children and teenagers. There was less concern that insufficient priority is given to ensuring young people's physical safety or that children and teenagers are not provided with enough opportunities for leisure activities.
- Over half the young people felt they have enough things to do most of the time. However, age made a clear difference and older

children showed the most dissatisfaction. Girls also seemed less satisfied than boys, and children from 'Other ethnicity' backgrounds were less satisfied than those describing themselves as 'White'.

• Children had lots of ideas about how adults could improve young people's lives, but they could also see what they could do to make adults' lives happier and more enjoyable.

TEN

Findings and messages

Children and young people, as well as adults with and without their own children, have lent their voices to the narratives of earlier chapters. Their views have helped to illuminate how childhood is constructed in contemporary England, how children and adults regard and respond to each other, and different perspectives on priorities for young lives. The research sample in question comprised some 2,000 young people from 7 to 15 years and 500 adults. These respondents were drawn from the general population and provided a 'normal' range of views. Undoubtedly they included some young people and families in difficulty, but those with particular problems were not specifically targeted and will not have been numerous. This final chapter draws out key messages for policy and practice that start with, but go beyond, what they said. These messages assume that policy and practice must be for all children, including those with problems of different kinds. However they must take account of the enormous individual differences between children but yet seek to bring different worlds of childhood together in the interests of social cohesion and the commonality of citizenship. The goal must also be to reduce inequalities within childhood, and to investigate and act on their causes and impacts as a matter of urgency. It is hoped these messages will resonate not only with policy makers and practitioners but also with children and adults themselves.

Children want to be children

A first clear conclusion is that children, young and old, want to be children. Almost all those in the surveys described their childhoods as happy, most said they enjoyed being young, and only a minority reported a lot to worry about. Indeed, the main 'best thing' about being young was not having many worries and responsibilities.

For all these reasons, most children were not in any hurry to become young adults and many thought children and young people grow up too quickly. Well over half felt they had to make too many decisions for themselves (although there was no indication how many is too many). They wanted to grow up, have their say, and be listened to and involved in the process of their own lives – but in their own time. Part of being a child is getting older, gaining more responsibility and trust, earning money, and generally becoming more independent, preferably in a setting where there are parents and families to fall back on.

This is not to ignore the many thousands of children, not included within the surveys, who live extremely unhappy and deprived lives. Poverty, racism and deprivation have certainly not gone away, large numbers of children continue to be physically and sexually abused, considerable proportions suffer mental health problems at some time during their childhoods, many experience serious traumas of one kind or another, and thousands have childhoods that make them unhappy in yet other ways. All these young people might enthusiastically share the views of children in our survey if they did not have other priorities in their lives. Our goal must be to strive to minimise their difficulties and enable them, too, to enjoy being young and growing up.

Few children, however, regard childhood as all good news. Even happy young people do not like everything about being young, and those in the surveys felt they had things to grumble about – in particular, feeling restricted, having to go to school, getting told off, having to do things they disliked, and not always being taken seriously. Their message was clear. Let them be children while they can, and let them be carefree. They wanted opportunities to have their say, and become involved in decisions affecting their daily lives, but they did not want to have to take undue responsibility too early. Let them judge for themselves when and how quickly they grow up.

Growing up and growing independence

Children do, nonetheless, have views on when most young people are ready for the transition from childhood to adulthood and prepared to take on greater responsibilities. Older children (those at primary school level were not asked) in the survey suggested the ages at which they felt young people might want to become independent in four specific areas. On average, they thought they should be legally responsible for their own behaviour and actions by the age of 14, learn about sex and relationships at 11, be able to visit a doctor for a confidential appointment at just over 13, and baby-sit for another family's children at about 14-and-a-half. On the whole, adults were in broad agreement.

The UN Committee on the Rights of the Child (2002) recommends a significant rise in the age of criminal responsibility across the UK. The views of young people and adults in the study lent support to this idea by suggesting that 14 years is a suitable age to take legal responsibility for one's own behaviour. This is a key message for legal reform. Graham (2004) has further suggested that 14 years might be taken as a more general point of transition from childhood to most adult responsibilities and adult rights. He advocates a ceremony to mark this transition near the beginning of the school year in which young people prepare for public examinations, and stresses the need for widespread preparation and education were such a proposal to be adopted.

Different roles and responsibilities require varying levels of skill and volition, and it is probably unsurprising that there is, in law, no single point of transition from childhood to adulthood. Growing up may be formalised by celebrations at 18 or 21 years, but these are symbolic rather than real boundaries. The lack of a formal rite of passage did not seem to be problematic for the children and adults in the surveys who thought that legal or recommended ages for behaviours examined were, in fact, about right.

Even so, all children are different – in their wishes and levels of maturity. Gillick competence (see pages 44–45) has been acknowledged as a useful principle in many areas that go beyond consent to medical treatment. The recognition of individual needs and capabilities is important in any situation in which young people are involved in decisions about their own lives.

Protection and freedom

Children want to be able to make their own choices, but they also enjoy some degree of protection. This can create an apparent conflict as well as blurred lines about who should make decisions about what. Interventions bring taunts of 'Nanny State' and invasion of family privacy, but failing to protect children's health and well-being is equally deplored. The result is an inevitable compromise and piecemeal tinkering exemplified in the current battle over what young people eat. Children's poor diets are criticised, parents are challenged to re-impose authority, and the state is urged to set standards. And, amid all this, we stress the right of children to have a say.

Tensions between protection and freedom also arise where children's safety is concerned. Feeling safe emerged as extremely important to children in our study, and was indeed their number one concern for public policy. Nonetheless they felt that adults worry too much about them hurting themselves or being in danger. The young people clearly voiced the message that they need and want increasing opportunities to experience risk and make their own decisions.

This may not be easy in the current climate where just thinking about children's safety can spawn something akin to panic. Not only are worries about traffic danger and stranger danger commonly voiced, but now we regularly also hear about the perils of mobile phones, school trips, Internet encounters, adventure playgrounds, heavy school bags, power lines and radio transmitters, sunbathing, drugs and inoculations, as well as playing conkers and wearing tinsel at Christmas. The impression is that nothing much is safe. Recently published research (reported in *The Guardian*, 30 July 2004) even suggests that children who eat an apple or pear every day could be exceeding the pesticide safety threshold because of residues on fruit. The adults in the survey, like the children, cited protection of young people as a clear number one priority policy area.

The current emphasis on safety and the accompanying fears seem to mean that children's lives are in many ways more restricted than previously. A report published by Demos and the Green Alliance (2004) suggests that most 10- and 11-year-olds stay at home rather than play outside because of fears ranging from traffic to terrorist attack, and around four in ten primary school and two in ten secondary school children are regularly taken to school by car. When away from home children may remain under surveillance (Garrett, 2004) and be watched by CCTV cameras, tracked through their mobile phones, or issued with tagging devices that allow parents to know where they are at all times. None of this is helping children to learn to cope with risk and incorporate it within their lives. Indeed, it may be encouraging them to engage in far more dangerous activities as parks and playgrounds become increasingly boring and offer fewer challenges and excitement.

The Play Safety Forum (2004), comprising the main national organisations in England with an interest in safety and children's play, endorses children's needs and wishes to take risks when they play, and stresses how play provision must manage the level of risk so that children are not exposed to unacceptable risks of death or serious injury. The government has pledged to tackle a range of 'safety and security' themes such as making neighbourhoods safer and encouraging walking and cycling, but these do not yet go far enough in giving a challenge back to children. It is hoped, however, that the current strategic play programme, which will offer local authorities funding for public space planning provided they embed play within their wider policy framework and engage with young people in developing new provision (CABE Space, 2004), will make a difference in the future. Challenging and supervised adventure playgrounds have been demonstrated to be attractive to young people up to 19 years, especially if they are involved in their development, and many more are called for. Britain is rich in green spaces and it is to be hoped that parks and woodlands across the land will be adapted into places where young people can encounter risk yet remain safe.

Encouraging risk is important for young people's well-being not only in developing crucial personal survival skills, but also in promoting useful social skills. If the government continues to pursue an agenda of entrepreneurship and globalisation, which in turn demands risk taking and competition in individuals, it is essential that risk-taking opportunities are provided to young people during their most formative years.

Behaviour and its control

Young people in the surveys reinforced the view that there is currently a lack of places for them to go, and a shortage of activities they enjoy and can afford: about half said that only sometimes are there enough activities available. Inevitably this situation contributes to the 'antisocial' labels they commonly attract. Groups of teenagers 'hanging around' may seem threatening to adults, and indeed half the adults in the study said they sometimes feel threatened by such groups in public places. Furthermore, over four in ten adults strongly agreed that children's and teenagers' behaviour is not controlled strictly enough, and almost the same number again slightly agreed.

A number of approaches are important to dispel these tensions within the general population as well as to deal with the antisocial behaviour presented by a minority of young people. First, the solution is in part to refute common myths about young people while at the same time acknowledging that there is a real problem. Although there has been a recent rise in gang culture (Beebee, 2004), and nearly one in four 15- and 16-year-olds admits to carrying a weapon (Schopen, 2005), real 'troublemakers' comprise only a small proportion of their age group and are particularly likely to be located in certain neighbourhoods. Furthermore, while findings from the 2003 Crime and Justice Survey revealed that four in ten 14- to 16-year-olds said they had committed at least one act of antisocial behaviour in the past year, in most cases this involved causing a 'public disturbance' or annoying neighbours (Hayward and Sharp, 2005). Stereotypes of young people as unruly and out of order are, for the main part, unjustified and, as Alderson (2004) points out, our children deserve better than to be written off as a group decent people need to be protected from.

It is not enough to acknowledge, as observed by Pearson (1983), that all generations are similar in whingeing about youth. The task at hand is to convey the message that 'most kids are okay' and to encourage tolerance across the generations. While the British Crime Survey (Wood, 2004) reported that 28% of adults saw 'teenagers hanging around' as a 'very big' or 'fairly big' problem in their local area, it has also to be recognised that such behaviour is an important social activity for many teenagers (Moore, 2003/04). As younger children in areas characterised by high deprivation and crime are also likely to point to teenagers as the cause of much nuisance and antisocial behaviour (Camina, 2004), it seems that these messages need to reach all age groups.

A second priority is to provide young people with more things they like doing. The recent Green Paper on *Youth matters* (DfES, 2005) has addressed this issue and pledged to provide more activities and better places for young people to go. As well as establishing an 'opportunity fund' in each local authority to be spent on local projects that young people want, it proposes to encourage more young people to volunteer and become involved in their communities, and to support local authorities in developing and piloting 'opportunity cards' to provide discounts (which could be withheld or increased, depending on young people's behaviour) for local activities. It is too early to know how well these measures will be implemented and work, but it is hoped that they will be a step in the right direction. A particular challenge is to provide physical activities that appeal to girls (Bailey et al, 2005).

In addition, there need to be strategies to prevent, discourage and deal with antisocial behaviour. Early family interventions such as Sure Start, involving multiagency support where and when needed, are a valuable starting point. Current attempts to encourage a law-abiding and socially cohesive society, which tries to bridge difficulties not only between young people and adults but also between different groups of young people, are also important. These strategies aim to encourage young people to see themselves as citizens with responsibilities, and to engender a commonality between young people while continuing to value their individuality. An emphasis on the Citizenship curriculum, reassurance policing, and strategies such as youth offending teams and other multiagency partnerships including the police, are some of the approaches taken (Stenson, 2005). There is, however, an urgent need to assess the effectiveness of these measures (Lovell, 2005).

Many measures to encourage social order among young people focus on the individual but may well be more effective were they to urge community responsibility, and the involvement of families and children, to a much greater degree. They are also often accompanied by penalties. All political parties now favour tough measures for young people who are 'out of order', and the past years have seen the introduction of dispersal zones, Acceptable Behaviour Contracts (ABCs), Anti-Social Behaviour Orders (Asbos) and on-the-spot fines as well as an increase in the use of custodial sentences for young people. Although it remains to be seen what impact such punitive measures have, it seems unlikely that they will meet with much success unless the broader context in which many young people live is taken into account. There are enormous inequalities based on class and ethnicity in our society and many young people struggle to grow up in the face of intergenerational conflict as well as animosity from within their own age group. Imposing authority within such a context is missing the point.

Furthermore, and for young people more generally, social cohesion and responsible citizenship can carry an implication of conformity to social norms and may not be in line with young people's own ideas of lifestyle and individuality. Children and teenagers are likely to feel they are social actors with their own script to follow rather than malleable minors. They may also have their own ideas about community and responsibility that are at odds with those of adults. This discrepancy can make childhood seem problematic from an adult perspective.

Antisocial behaviour is but a shorthand for a wide range of actions undertaken for a wide range of reasons. Muncie (2004) points out how "adult anxiety has consistently been expressed in terms of youthful vulnerability, nuisance and misbehaviour and has focused on the simply undesirable, worrying and disobedient as well as criminality". This has been implicitly acknowledged by the 1998 Crime and Disorder Act and the 2003 Antisocial Behaviour Act which focus as much on the 'antisocial' as on the 'criminal'. Surely it is time to reverse this trend and to make much stronger distinctions between behaviour that is genuinely detrimental to society and that which we just do not like?

The public presentation of childhood

Negative views of youth are promoted by public images that fail to acknowledge that childhood refers to the collective of individual children who are all different. Sensationalised images of youth predominate in the media and elsewhere, and display bias in the behaviour they report as well as the status of the children they depict.

The well-behaved, well-adjusted, 'ordinary' child may not be newsworthy, but this does not explain the undue attention paid to negative messages about youth. The challenge is to rectify the balance if these messages are not to infiltrate the public consciousness and thereby endure.

The adults in the study seemed in little doubt that the portrayal of young people in the media is predominantly negative, and confirmed the need for much more realistic and consistent messages. Were they aware, however, that they themselves may indeed be reinforcing these messages? It has already been noted that large numbers of adults regard children and teenagers as badly controlled. In addition, parents in the study consistently described their own children in a much more favourable light than children in general, especially when it came to being respectful enough to adults. Although it may simply be that they see themselves as good parents, this observation does highlight an inherent contradiction in attitudes towards childhood. While on the one hand adults suggest the media are predominantly negative towards young people, on the other hand they appear to be (perhaps inadvertently) conveying similar messages themselves. It is likely that there is a vicious circle at play with media messages both influencing and being reinforced by adult attitudes.

Not only are adult attitudes influenced by media messages, however, but young people's own self-image can also be affected. Children may seek out advice or role models and become confused by the way the messages are at odds with other priorities in their lives. In some ways the voices of the children reported in this study reinforce the view. A plea has been heard to let them be children while they can, while allowing them independence and responsibility as they mature. Let them decide how they want to dress and wear their hair; let them make mistakes for themselves. At the same time, make them feel safe, physically and emotionally, and ensure they know they are valued.

If children are to be allowed to be children, change is needed: in the public presentation of childhood, for policy and practice towards young people, for manufacturers of consumer goods, for advertising and promotion, for television and the media. It is hard enough growing up without added unwarranted pressures that may have a damaging effect through the cultivation of unfair attitudes. The International Federation of Journalists drew up guidelines and principles for reporting on issues involving children that were adopted by journalists' organisations from 70 countries in 1998. Among other things, these state that journalists should, in particular, "avoid the use of stereotypes and sensational presentation to promote journalistic material involving children". It could also be suggested that the media make a greater effort to cover issues raised directly by young people rather than being over-reliant on the agenda of politicians and other adults.

There are also some interesting examples of initiatives to promote positive images of children and young people (for example, Goddard, 2004; Cushion, 2005; NCB, 2003). Generally speaking, however, Professor Rod Morgan, head of the Youth Justice Board, has reported that young people are "really unhappy about the overwhelming negative images of them in the media" and suggested that we should stop using the word 'yob' in relation to young people (reported in *The Guardian*, 23 May 2005). Being more respectful, in this sense, would be a good start.

It is also held that much of the concern about 'respect', 'thugs', and 'antisocial behaviour' represents coded references to the behaviour of certain groups of young people. These might be those from certain ethnic, religious or cultural groups, or they might be poor children and young people brought up by carers perceived to have inadequate parenting skills. Not only the social cohesion agenda, but also initiatives such as Sure Start, the plethora of parenting programmes for families at risk (Barrett, 2003), and the Citizenship curriculum, are based in part on these views.

A question of 'respect'

Respect, nonetheless, is a highly contested concept. At one extreme, it invokes the idea of fear and intimidation for the violent, the powerful and the strong as witnessed, for instance, by the themes and values embodied in 'gangsta rap'. At another level, the government is currently using the term to refer to antisocial behaviour in its attempt to shore up traditional authority in the home and the community. This interpretation also implies a level of coercion in that there are sanctions for those who fail to show respect for individuals as well as for rules and prescribed values. At the bottom line, respect may be defined in terms of values and voluntary behaviour. Respect, in this sense, is not essentially based on coercion, even if authority is involved, but is more to do with courtesy, consideration and esteem shown by one person towards another.

This last definition is likely to be closest to the understanding children and adults in the surveys had when we asked about respect across the generations – of children for adults and of adults for children. Some interesting findings emerged. For instance, both generations felt that young people were less likely to be polite and respectful towards adults than adults were towards them. They were also in agreement that young people were less likely to talk and listen to their parents than vice versa, and that young people enjoyed doing things with adults less than the other way round. Children seemed quite willing to acknowledge their own 'shortcomings'. They were prepared to indicate that they are not always as polite and respectful to adults as they might be, and some acknowledged that they could not demand respect from adults if they do not give it in return. Their comments about how adults and young people could make each other's lives happier reinforce this general point. These included adults making sure they pay young people due respect, being friendly and welcoming, listening, and taking children's views into account.

If respect is to be variously interpreted, then measures to tackle disrespect also need to be broadly based. It may, for instance, be up to the state to come up with some of the answers. Its response so far has been to suggest that the 'respect' agenda should involve such measures as intelligence-led community policing, increased discipline in schools, greater use of Asbos, and restoration of a 'culture of decency'. *The Express* (12 May 2005) has, in this vein, launched a crusade to "instil respect, self-discipline and a genuine sense of community" in Britain's youth, and is calling on ministers to back a new national service that would require all school leavers to complete a period of community work from a range of options, including caring for older people, disabled or sick people, helping in schools or improving the environment.

The question, nonetheless, is the impact such measures will have. There is a view that an essential element of any strategy must be to show young people respect in order to encourage them to respect others. This reiterates the point about not labelling them as 'thugs' and 'louts' and giving them a chance. If children and adults alike could be urged to pay lip service to 'respect', this would at least be a start. Adults need to remember what it was like to be a child, but they also need to recognise that youth culture has changed since they were young and that young people's current interests in crime, gun culture, music and gigs, fashion, mobiles, drugs, sex and cars (Barham, 2004) may not all have been their own. The other side of the picture is that young people need to have an insight into the meaning of adulthood. Although parenting can be stressful (Edwards and Gillies, 2004), particularly during the teenage years (Edwards, 2004), parents frequently feel isolated and unsupported. To make matters worse, a recent survey of 1,678 adults (Millie et al, 2005) found that two in three blamed parents for antisocial behaviour. There seems to be a message that adults and young people all need to be more understanding.

The generation game

Children and adults belong to different generations, and intergenerational issues arise through both their interactions and their differences. The children and adults taking part in the surveys were born decades apart and exposed to different cultures, histories, knowledge and experiences as they grew up. This study has highlighted some of the ways in which such differences seem to affect intergenerational patterns and relations.

First, there was a clear impression that, on the whole, young people and adults do not get on too badly and actually enjoy doing things together. Families are important to most young people who said that spending time with them, and being looked after and paid attention, are among the best things about growing up. Those who felt somewhat deprived in this sense said they would like adults to listen to them and take their views into account more often. Parents were also an important influence on their children, and indeed rather more than they might believe. While children and teenagers tended to say that family and parents have the greatest influence on young people, adults seemed to think that friends and peer pressure are more important. This must be an important and reassuring message for parents.

Second, although it is common practice to say how things are different now from in the past, this research suggests that while some things seem to change, others do not. Adults, for instance, were just as likely as young people to say their childhoods were happy, but much more often reported a strict upbringing. Asked to point to ways that childhood had changed since they were young, nine in ten adults indicated that 'children and teenagers have to grow up too quickly' more often nowadays, and most thought that young people's views are taken into account more now than previously. Furthermore, over half felt children are more protected these days, and half thought that young people lead more carefree lives. Although there was less agreement among adults about whether or not parents have changed much in terms of how much they talk with their children, the most common feeling was that things are much the same as ever.

Third, relations between the generations are not static and change over time. Age affected the relationships young people felt they have with adults, and as they get older they are less likely to think they talk to each other enough or listen to each other properly, and they do not enjoy being with each other as much: adults become less significant in children's day-to-day lives, and the influence of friends increases. As young people grow up, they are also less likely to say that most adults are friendly towards them or welcome children playing in their neighbourhood. With increasing age, young people become less sure that England is a good place to grow up in. The need to feel cared for and valued is mentioned less, and greater emphasis is placed on being allowed a say.

Changing relationships between the generations are a normal part of growing up. All the same, one message that comes through from the research is that both young people and adults wished that they did more things together. For children such as those in the surveys, promoting family-friendly employment policies, and making it easier for the generations to spend time together, may be one effective strategy. Work–life balance has changed considerably over even the past decade (Barrett, 2004), and four in ten families with dependent children and at least one working parent includes a parent who regularly works at weekends (Barnes and Bryson, 2004). Coordinating childcare, schooling and employment can present parents with enormous challenges (Skinner, 2005), and many existing measures to promote a better work–life balance are, in effect, aimed at mothers (Hunt and Wallace, 2004). What is really needed are flexible measures that promote more equal sharing of family tasks between parents. In line with the philosophy of the *Youth matters* Green Paper, these should be driven much more than previously by a wish to meet the needs of children and young people.

For those in the surveys, too, perhaps the 1989 NSPCC advert with a small parent sitting on his child's lap, with the strapline 'Sit down and have a long listen to your kids', still has currency. For other young people and families, the answer may not be so easy. Addressing differences in attitude and culture – and sometimes the alienation – between generations of families from some ethnic, religious and cultural backgrounds provide a particular challenge in this respect.

Children are not all the same

Findings from the research highlight the difficulty in talking about young people as if they are all the same. Childhood is an individual experience and children are no more alike than adults. Generalisations about 'children' and 'young people' should be used with care.

Age is an important factor influencing the meaning of childhood and some of the differences that emerged from the surveys have been highlighted above. Gender also makes a difference. At primary school level, boys were less likely than girls to say they are happy, and twice as likely to say their parents are strict. At all ages, girls were more likely than boys to think parents and carers are over-protective. Boys were also more likely than girls to say they have things to worry about. On the other hand, girls were most likely to say children and young people grow up too quickly. Intriguingly, boys felt they should become responsible for their actions, have confidential medical appointments and, particularly, learn about sex and relationships at an earlier age than did girls.

Ethnicity is also important. Although the findings must be viewed with caution as the small number of children who described themselves in ways other than 'White' have been grouped together, some differences did nonetheless emerge. For example, 'White' children were more likely than these 'Other ethnicity' children to say that most adults are polite enough to them, and more likely at primary school level (but not secondary school level) to find most adults friendly to young people of their age. 'White' females, but not males, are also most likely to feel welcome in public places. 'Other ethnicity' children had a greater tendency to say they are brought up strictly and, for males but not females, to suggest that young people grow up too quickly. Children from 'Other ethnicity' backgrounds were most likely to say they do not have enough things to do. In addition, 'White' children seemed prepared to grow up sooner and recommend lower ages for taking criminal responsibility, confidential medical appointments, and learning about sex and relationships.

Perhaps the main conclusion from these findings is the need to recognise and acknowledge individual differences based on group characteristics such as gender and ethnicity (Madge, 2001). This presents a particular challenge for the social cohesion agenda that must have an emphasis on both the commonality of issues facing young people as well as the distinctions. This imperative gains ever greater priority as society becomes increasingly diverse and as new social issues are highlighted. For instance, and following the July 2005 London bombings, it has been suggested that older Muslim generations have failed to recognise the 'identity crisis' faced by members of the younger generations. Issues surrounding the impact of ethnicity, religion and culture are complex and can at once straddle both generational and social divides. The serious challenge for policy and the state is to provide the framework for a common citizenship model based on normative practices that incorporate rights, duties and values. There is a need to engender a commonality among young people based on being British without the requirement to abandon key elements of individual culture and heritage.

England could be more child friendly

Children have mixed views about whether England is a good country to grow up in. Most of those in the surveys, whatever their age, were likely to say that it is quite good rather than very good. Nonetheless, primary school level children were more positive than older children, and this supports the finding that adults were more likely to think England is friendly towards children than towards teenagers. One message is surely that child-friendly activities must apply to all age groups of young people, and to everyone regardless of background or circumstances.

When asked why they think England is (or is not) a good country to grow up in, children were generally agreed that it meets most needs, provides good education and other services, is generally safe, has people who are kind and friendly, and gives plenty of opportunities for things to do. What they did not like were aspects of the environment, crime, vandalism, danger and dirt. Older children also pointed to a shortage of amenities and activities that are free. Nonetheless, only a minority said that most adults are friendly towards them (and this proportion drops with age), and most recognised that some are friendly and others are not. Well over half the children, however, say they feel welcome in public places, such as shops and leisure centres, most of the time. Reassuringly, fewer than one in ten said they do 'not very often' feel welcome in public places. It is perhaps worth taking note that the findings, tentative though they may be in this respect, suggest that children who described themselves as from 'Other ethnicity' backgrounds encounter England as less friendly than those from 'White' backgrounds.

Much play takes place in streets, parks and other public areas. Young people and adults were asked about adult reactions in these settings. Views were again inconsistent, although adults tended to be the most positive. Most said they enjoy seeing children playing in their neighbourhood, and this was particularly true of parents. These views may, nonetheless, conceal differences in adult attitudes to younger children and teenagers. They may also fail to identify differing reactions to groups of young people distinguished by circumstances, ethnicity or culture.

More adults (and over half of all mothers) think England is less child friendly than other countries, than think it is more child friendly.

They see other countries as more welcoming towards children, cherishing them more, and treating them better. They feel that England is less tolerant and less family-orientated. Those who saw England as more child friendly than elsewhere mentioned abuse abroad, the better facilities and higher standard of living in England, and the fact that this country is more democratic. While these findings may in part reflect the likelihood that adults were basing their foreign experiences on their holidays, they should also act as a sharp reminder that we may not always be as child friendly as we could be.

Meeting the challenges

The passage to adulthood is long and winding and young people need to negotiate the pathway in their own time. All children are different, and while some may prefer to charge on, others will choose to take it more slowly. Some will want to take extra risks, and some will need special protection and guidance. And while for many growing up will be a positive experience conducted against a backcloth of general contentment and support, there are those for whom it will occur under much more stressful conditions.

There is evidently a role for families and the state in the promotion of childhood. Children and young people need advocates and support, and they want good facilities and services. There is also a need for workable and effective policies to reduce inequalities and disadvantage. The encouraging news is that children are much more in the public eye than ever before. England now has a Minister for Children as well as a Children's Commissioner, and there is more and more legislation to protect young interests together with a growing priority to consult children on a wide range of matters. We now recognise their capabilities, rights and responsibilities, and we have seen the benefits of their involvement in community life and in decisions that affect them. Children have moved on, but they are not mini-adults. One task is to ensure that they are able to experience childhood while they have the chance, and to make sure that they are not simply being prepared to be productive adults.

Another task, however, is to make sure that all young people, and especially the most alienated, feel 'connected' as young citizens. A broad strategy, rather than a series of piecemeal gestures, is called for that brings young people together but does not expect them all to be the same. Not only the social cohesion agenda, but also the recent 2004 Children Act, *Every child matters*, and *Youth matters*, go some way in setting a framework and advocating measures and approaches. Success will, however, depend on making direct contact with young people, and it seems that Hewitt's (2005) call for much more youth work and mentoring is timely. He points out that there is a dearth of well-resourced youth work in the UK, and that what is needed is a professional service that is based on detailed local understanding as well as a close knowledge of young people themselves. Not only could this help to prevent many young people drifting into antisocial behaviour, but it could also create opportunities for inspiring a sense of human community and common citizenship.

Addressing the divide between young people and adults is another clear priority. In most individual cases this is no serious issue as children and their carers get on well. Even in the happiest families, however, there is a sense that both younger and older generations could be more considerate and attentive towards each other. Creative ideas on how this could be encouraged are only to be welcomed.

Successful childhoods depend, too, on a lack of tension between images of childhood, the state and what children think and want. The paradox of childhood is that it means taking responsibility for young people, but also letting young people take responsibility for themselves.

References

Alderson, P. (1993) *Children's consent to surgery*, Buckingham: Open University Press.

Alderson, P. (2004) 'Guilty of being young', *The Guardian*, 22 June, p 18.

Aries, P. (1962) *Centuries of childhood: A social history of family life* (translated by Robert Baldick), London: Cape.

Aynsley-Green, A. (2003) 'The child first and always – is it?', The inaugural Great Ormond Street Hospital lecture, London: Great Ormond Street Hospital for Children NHS Trust.

Bailey, R., Wellard, I. and Dismore, H. (2005) 'Girls and physical activities: a summary review', *Education and Health*, vol 23, no 1, pp 3-5.

Balding, J. (2002) *Young people in 2001: The health-related behaviour questionnaire results for 15,881 young people between the ages of 10 and 15*, Bristol: SHEU.

Balding, J., Regis, D. and Wise, A. (1998) *No worries? Young people and mental health*, Bristol: SHEU.

Ball, M. (1998) *School inclusion: The school, the family and the community*, York: Joseph Rowntree Foundation.

Barham, N. (2004) *Disconnected: Why our kids are turning their backs on everything we thought we knew*, London: Ebury Press.

Barker, M. and Petley, J. (eds) (1997) *Ill effects: The media/violence debate*, London: Routledge.

Barnes, M. and Bryson, C. (2004) *Keep time for children: The incidence of weekend working*, London: NCSR.

Barrett, H. (2003) *Parenting programmes for families at risk: A source book*, London: NFPI.

Barrett, H. (2004) *UK family trends 1994-2004*, London: NFPI.

Becker, F. (2001) 'The links between child abuse and animal abuse', NSPCC Information Briefings (available at www.nspcc.org.uk/inform).

Becker, F. and French, L. (2004) 'Making the links: child abuse, animal cruelty and domestic violence', *Child Abuse Review*, vol 13, no 6, pp 399-414.

Beebee, S. (2004) 'Gang culture', *Shabaab*, no 39, January, pp 22-3.

Beresford, P. (2002) 'Maturity needed', *Community Care*, no 1430, 11 July, p 20.

Borland, M., Laybourn, A., Hill, M. and Brown, J. (1998) *Middle childhood: The perspectives of children and parents*, London: Jessica Kingsley Publishers.

Bossard, J.H.S. (1948) *The sociology of child development*, New York: Harper & Row.

Bradshaw, J. (2002) 'Child poverty and child outcomes', *Children & Society*, vol 16, no 2, pp 131-40.

Brannen, J. (2004) 'Childhoods across the generations: stories from women in four-generation English families', *Childhood*, vol 11, no 4, pp 409-28.

Brannen, J., Heptinall, E. and Bhopal, K. (2000) *Connecting children: Care and family life in later childhood*, London: RoutledgeFalmer.

Brown, S. (2003) *Crime and law in media culture*, Buckingham: Open University Press.

BT/ChildLine (2002) *Are young people being heard?*

Buckingham, D. (2000) *After the death of childhood: Growing up in the age of electronic media*, Cambridge: The Polity Press.

Bussmann, K.-D. (2004) 'Evaluating the subtle impact of a ban on corporal punishment of children in Germany', *Child Abuse Review*, vol 13, no 5, pp 292-311.

Butler, I., Robinson, M. and Scanlan, L. (2005) *Children and decision-making*, London: NCB for the Joseph Rowntree Foundation.

CABE Space (2004) *What would you do with this space? Involving young people in the design and care of urban spaces*, London: CABE Space.

Camina, M. (2004) *Understanding and engaging deprived communities*, London: Home Office.

Cawson, P. (2002) *Child maltreatment in the family: The experience of a national sample of young people*, London: NSPCC.

Children's Society and Children's Play Council (2002) Research carried out to mark National Playday on 7 August (reported at http://news.bbc.co.uk/1/low/education/2158711.stm).

Clark, A. and Moss, P. (2001) *Listening to children: The Mosaic approach*, London: NCB.

Creighton, S. and Russell, N. (1995) *Voices from childhood: A survey of childhood experiences and attitudes to child rearing among adults in the United Kingdom*, London: NSPCC.

Cullingford, C. (1997) 'Parents from the point of view of their children', *Educational Review*, vol 49, no 1, pp 47-56.

Curtis, N. (2002) 'When Harry met "Arry"', *Evening Standard*, 15 January.

Cushion, S. (2005) 'Positive politics', *Young People Now*, no 277, 6 April, p 18.

CYPU (Children and Young People's Unit) (2001) *Building a strategy for children and young people*, London: CYPU.

Darwin, C. (1877) 'A biographical sketch of an infant', *Mind*, vol 2, pp 285-94.

Davin, A. (1999) 'What is a child?', in A. Fletcher and S. Hussey (eds) *Childhood in question: Children, parents and the state*, Manchester: Manchester University Press, pp 15-36.

de Mause, L. (ed) (1976) *The history of childhood: The evolution of parent–child relationships as a factor in history*, London: Souvenir Press.

Demos and Green Alliance (2004) *A child's place: Why environment matters to children*, London: Demos and Green Alliance.

DfEE (Department for Education and Employment) (2000) *Sex and relationship education guidance*, London: DfEE.

DfES (Department for Education and Skills) (2003) *Every child matters*, London: DfES.

DfES (2005) *Youth matters*, London: DfES.

DH (Department of Health) (2003) *National service framework for children, young people and maternity services*, London: DH.

Edwards, L. (2004) *The Lever Faberge family report 2004*, London: IPPR.

Edwards, R. and Gillies, V. (2004) 'Support in parenting: values and consensus concerning who to turn to', *Journal of Social Policy*, vol 33, no 4, pp 627-47.

Electoral Commission (2004) *Age of electoral majority: Report and recommendations*, London: Electoral Commission.

Ellis, S. (1843) *The mothers of England, their influence and responsibility*, New York: D. Appleton.

Ericson, R. (1995) *Crime and the media*, Brookfield, VT: Dartmouth.

Essau, C.A. (2004) 'Risk-taking behaviour among German adolescents', *Journal of Youth Studies*, vol 7, no 4, pp 499-512.

Fenwick, E. and Smith, T. (1993) *Adolescence: The survival guide for parents and teenagers*, London: Dorling Kindersley.

Fionda, J. (ed) (2001) *Legal concepts of childhood*, Oxford: Hart Publishing.

Flood, S. (2002) 'Having their say', *Young Minds Magazine*, no 59, p 31.

Flouri, E., Buchanan, A., Welsh, E. and Lewis, J. (2004) *Father's involvement with their secondary-school-aged children: Summary of findings*, York: Joseph Rowntree Foundation.

Franklin, A. and Madge, N. (2000) *In our view: Children, teenagers and parents talk about services for young people*, London: NCB.

Frean, A. (2002) 'Boomerang kids can't give up home comforts', *The Times*, 21 March.

Freeman, M. (ed) (2001) *Lloyd's introduction to jurisprudence* (7th edn), London: Sweet and Maxwell.

Furedi, F. (2001) *Paranoid parenting: Abandon your anxieties and be a good parent*, London: Allen Lane.

Garrett, P.M. (2004) 'The electronic eye: emerging surveillant practices in social work with children and families', *European Journal of Social Work*, vol 7, no 1, pp 57-71.

Ghate, D. and Daniels, A. (1997) *Talking about my generation: A survey of 8-15 year olds growing up in the 1990s*, NSPCC Policy, Practice, Research Series, London: NSPCC.

Ghate, D., Hazel, N., Creighton, S., Finch, S. and Field, J. (2003) *The national study of parents, children and discipline in Britain. Summary of key findings*, London: Policy Research Bureau.

Giddens, A. (1998) *The third way*, Cambridge: The Polity Press.

Gillies, V., Ribbens McCarthy, J. and Holland, J. (2001) *Pulling together, pulling apart: The family lives of young people*, London: Family Policy Studies Centre for the Joseph Rowntree Foundation.

Gittins, D. (1998) *The child in question*, Basingstoke: Macmillan.

GLA (Greater London Authority) (2004) *Making London better for all children and young people: The Mayor's children and young people's strategy*, London: GLA.

Goddard, C. (2004) 'Who are you calling a yob?', *Young People Now*, no 254, 13 October, pp 16-17.

Graham, P. (2004) *The end of adolescence*, Oxford: Oxford University Press.

Gram, M. (2004) 'The future world champions? Ideals for upbringing represented in contemporary European advertisements', *Childhood*, vol 11, no 3, August, pp 319-37.

Hall, D. (2003) 'Foreword', in RCPCH, *Bridging the gaps*, London: RCPCH.

Hallett, C. and Prout, A. (eds) (2003) *Hearing the voices of children: Social policy for a new century*, London: RoutledgeFalmer.

Hardyment, C. (1983) *Dream babies: Child care from Locke to Spock*, London: Jonathan Cape Ltd.

Hart, J. (2005) 'The young ones', *Horizons*, no 32, March, pp 24-5.

Hastings, G., Stead, M., McDermott, L., Forsyth, A., Mackintosh, A.M., Rayner, M., Godfrey, C., Caraher, M. and Angus, K. (2003) *Review of research on the effects of food promotion to children: Final report*, London: Foods Standards Agency.

Hayward, R. and Sharp, C. (2005) *Young people, crime and antisocial behaviour: Findings from the 2003 Crime and Justice Survey*, London: Home Office.

Hendrick, H. (1997) *Children, childhood and English society 1880-1990*, Cambridge: Cambridge University Press.

Hendrick, H. (2003) *Child welfare: Historical dimensions, contemporary debate*, Bristol: The Policy Press.

Henricson, C. (2000) *Teenagers' attitudes to parenting*, London: NFPI.

Hewitt, R. (2005) 'It is in the communities that these battles are won or lost', *The Guardian*, 20 July.

Hill, A. (2000) 'One girl in six hits puberty by age of eight', *The Observer*, 18 June, pp 1-2.

Hillman, M., Adams, J. and Whitelegg, J. (1990) *One false move ... A study of children's independent mobility*, London: PSI.

Holland, P. (1992) *What is a child?*, London: Virago.

Holland, P. (2004) *Picturing childhood: The myth of the child in popular imagery*, London: I.B. Tauris.

Home Office (1998) *Supporting families: A consultation document*, London: The Stationery Office.

House of Lords and House of Commons (2003) *Joint Committee on Human Rights – Sixth Report*, London: The Stationery Office.

Howitt, D. (1998) *Crime, the media and the law*, Chichester: John Wiley.

Hunt, J. and Wallace, C.J. (eds) (2004) 'Reconciliation between work and family life in the EU: reshaping gendered structures?', *Journal of Social Welfare and Family Law*, vol 26, no 3, pp 325-38.

Hutchby, I. and Moran-Ellis, J. (eds) (1998) *Children and social competence: Arenas of action*, London: Falmer Press.

IPPR (Institute for Public Policy Research) (2004) *Rethinking social justice*, London: IPPR.

James, A. and Prout, A. (eds) (1997) *Constructing and reconstructing childhood: Contemporary issues in the sociological study of childhood* (2nd edn), London: Falmer.

Jenks, C. (1996) *Childhood*, London: Routledge.

Jenks, C. (2001) 'Sociological perspectives and media representations of childhood', in J. Fionda (ed) *Legal concepts of childhood*, Oxford: Hart Publishing, pp 19-42.

Jones, G. and Bell, R. (2000) *Balancing acts: Youth, parenting and public policy*, York: Joseph Rowntree Foundation.

Katz, A. (1997) *The 'can do' girls: A barometer of change*, Oxford: Department of Applied Social Studies and Research, University of Oxford.

Katz, A. (1999) *Leading lads: 1,400 lads reveal what they really think about life in Britain today*, East Molesey: Young Voice.

Kidd-Hewitt, D. and Osborne, R. (eds) (1995) *Crime and the media: The post-modern spectacle*, London: Pluto Press.

Kirby, P., Lanyon, C., Cronin, K. and Sinclair, R. (2003) *Building a culture of participation: Involving children and young people in policy, service planning, delivery and evaluation*, London: DfES.

Langford, W., Lewis, C., Solomon, Y. and Warin, J. (2001) *Family understandings: Closeness, authority and independence in families with teenagers*, London: Family Policy Studies Centre for the Joseph Rowntree Foundation.

Larchner, V. (2005) 'ABC of adolescence: consent, competence, and confidentiality', *British Medical Journal*, vol 330, no 7487, 12 February, pp 353-6.

Leach, R. (2003) *Children's participation in family decision-making*, Highlight No 196, London: NCB.

Lee, N. (2001) *Childhood and society: Growing up in an age of uncertainty*, Buckingham: Open University Press.

Lewis, P. (2001) 'The medical treatment of children', in J. Fionda (ed) *Legal concepts of childhood*, Oxford: Hart Publishing, pp 151-164.

Lewis-Smith, V. (2003) 'Lazy, crude and callous TV', *Evening Standard*, 21 October.

Lindon, J. (1999) *Too safe for their own good? Helping children learn about risk and lifeskills*, London: National Early Years Network.

Lott, T. (2003) 'Children, you have never had it so good', *Evening Standard*, 3 July.

Lovell, E. (2005) 'Children and the use of anti-social behaviour orders', *Childright*, no 217, June, pp 14-16.

Madge, N. (2001) *Understanding difference: The meaning of ethnicity for young lives*, London: NCB.

Madge, N. and Franklin, A. (2003) *Change, challenge and school nursing*, London: NCB.

Mason, J. and Fattore, T. (eds) (2005) *Children taken seriously: In theory, policy and practice*, London: Jessica Kingsley Publishers.

Matthews, H. and Limb, M. (2000) *Exploring the 'fourth environment': Young people's use of place and views on their environment*, Children 5-16 Research Briefing No 9, Swindon: ESRC.

Matthews, H., Taylor, M., Percy-Smith, B. and Limb, M. (2000) 'The unacceptable *flaneur*: the shopping mall as a teenage hangout', *Childhood*, vol 7, no 3, pp 279-94.

Mayall, B. (2001) 'Understanding childhoods: a London study', in L. Alanen and B. Mayall (eds) *Conceptualising child–adult relations*, London: RoutledgeFalmer, pp 114-128.

Mayall, B. (2002) *Towards a sociology for childhood: Thinking from children's lives*, Buckingham: Open University Press.

McAllister, F. and Clarke, L. (1998) *Choosing childlessness*, London: Family Policy Studies Centre.

McKendrick, J.H., Bradford, M.G. and Fielder, A.V. (2000) 'Time for a party! Making sense of the commercialisation of leisure space for children', in S. Holloway and G. Valentine (eds) *Children's geography: Living, playing, learning*, London: Routledge, pp 100-18.

McNeish, H. and Roberts, H. (eds) (1995) *What works for children? Effective services for children and families*, Buckingham: Open University Press.

Measor, L. and Squires, P. (2000) *Young people and community safety: Inclusion, risk, tolerance and disorder*, Aldershot: Ashgate.

MHF (Mental Health Foundation) (1999) *The big picture: Promoting children and young people's mental health*, London: MHF.

Middleton, S., Ashworth, K. and Braithwaite, I. (1997) *Small fortunes: Spending on children, childhood poverty and parental sacrifice*, York: Joseph Rowntree Foundation.

Miles, T. (2002) 'Schools are told to tackle "sex is okay" magazines', *Evening Standard*, 30 April.

Millie, A., Jacobson, J., McDonald, E. and Hough, M. (2005) *Anti-social behaviour strategies: Finding a balance*, Bristol/York: The Policy Press for the Joseph Rowntree Foundation.

Mitchell, W., Bunton, R. and Green, E. (eds) (2004) *Young people, risk and leisure: Constructing identities in everyday life*, London: Palgrave Macmillan.

Montandon, C. (2001) 'The negotiation of influence: children's experience of parental educational practices in Geneva', in L. Alanen and B. Mayall (eds) *Conceptualising child–adult relations*, London: RoutledgeFalmer.

Moorcock, K. (1998) *Swings and roundabouts: The danger of safety in outdoor play environments*, Sheffield: Sheffield Hallam University Press.

Moore, S. (2003/04) 'Hanging about: the importance of bus-stop culture', *Youth and Policy*, no 82, Winter, pp 47-59.

MORI (2002) *Youth Survey 2002*, London: Youth Justice Board.

MORI (2004) Research carried out for *Young People Now*. http://www.mori.com/polls/2004/young-people-now.shtml

Morrow, V. (1998) *Understanding families: Children's perspectives*, London: NCB.

Morrow, V. (2000) 'We get played like fools: young people's accounts of community and institutional participation', in H. Ryan and J. Bull (eds) *Changing families, changing communities: Researching health and wellbeing among children and young people*, London: Health Development Agency.

Muncie,J. (2004) *Youth and crime* (2nd edn), London: Sage Publications.

NCB (National Children's Bureau) (2003) *Let's get positive. Challenging negative images of young people in care.* London: NCB.

NCB (National Children's Bureau) (2004) 'Insert: No abuse! Young people's views about smacking', *Loudspeaker*, no 8, July.

NCH Action for Children (1997) *Family forum. Family life: The age of anxiety*, London: NCH Action for Children.

NFPI (National Family and Parenting Institute) (2000) *Teenagers' attitudes to parenting: A survey of young people's experiences of being parented, and their views on how to bring up children*, London: NFPI.

NFPI (2003) *Hard sell, soft targets?*, London: NFPI.

O'Brien, M. (2000) *Childhood, urban space and citizenship: Child-sensitive urban regeneration*, Children 5-16 Research Briefing No 16, Swindon: ESRC.

Ofsted (2002) *Sex and relationships education in schools*, London: Ofsted.

Orme, N. (2001) *Medieval children*, New York and London: Yale University Press.

Pearson, C. (1983). *Hooligan: A history of respectable fears*, London: Macmillan.

Peek, L. (2000) 'One in six girls now reaches puberty aged eight', *The Times*, 19 June, p 3.

Phillips, M. (2005) 'Teenagers on family values', in A. Park (ed) *British social attitudes: The 21st report*, London: Sage Publications.

Play Safety Forum (2004) 'Managing risk in play provision: a position statement' (available at www.ncb.org.uk/cpc/res_detail.asp?id=279).

Posner, G.J. (1995) *The teenager's guide to the law*, London: Cavendish Publishing.

Postman, N. (1982) *The disappearance of childhood*, London: W.H. Allen.

Prout, A. (2005) *The future of childhood*, London: RoutledgeFalmer.

Qvortrup, J. (1991) *Childhood as a social phenomenon – An introduction to a series of national reports*, Eurosocial Report 36/1991, Vienna: European Centre.

Qvortrup, J. (1994) 'Childhood matters: an introduction', in J. Qvortrup, M. Bardy, G. Sgritta and H. Wintersberger (eds) *Childhood matters: Social theory, practice and politics*, Aldershot: Avebury Press, pp 1-23.

Raisingkids (2004) 'The National Family Mealtime Survey' (available at www.raisingkids.co.uk).

Reeves, R. (2003) 'The battle for childhood', *New Statesman*, 20 October, pp 18-20.

Revill, J. (2002) 'Now Barclays wants to give children credit cards', *Evening Standard*, 14 May.

Rousseau, J.-J. (1762) *Émile*, Paris. Duchesne.

Russell, I.M. (2005) *A national framework for youth action and engagement: Report of the Russell Commission*, London: Home Office.

Schopen, F. (2005) 'Lethal weapons', *Young People Now*, no 291, 13 July, pp 14-15.

Scott, S., Harden, J., Jackson, S. and Backett-Milburn, K. (2000) *The impact of risk and parental risk anxiety on the everyday worlds of children*, Children 5-16 Research Briefing No 19, Stirling: University of Stirling for the ESRC.

Sex Education Forum (2002) *Sex and relationships education for primary age children*, Forum Factsheet. London: NCB.

SHEU (Schools Health Education Unit) (2005) *Trends: Young people and emotional health and well-being 1983-2003*, Exeter: SHEU

Sinclair, R. (2004) 'Participation in practice: making it meaningful, effective and sustainable', *Children & Society*, vol 18, no 2, pp 106-18.

Sinclair, R., Cronin, K., Lanyon, C., Stone, V. and Hulusi, A. (2002) *Aim high, stay real: Outcomes for children and young people: The views of children, parents and practitioners*, London: CYPU.

Skinner, C. (2005) 'Coordination points: a hidden factor in reconciling work and family life', *Journal of Social Policy*, vol 34, no 1, January, pp 99-120.

Smith, J. (2002) 'Small fortune', *The Independent Review*, 7 May.

Smith, R. (2003) *Youth justice: Ideas, policy, practice*, Cullompton: Willan Publishing.

Spender, Q. and John, A. (2001) 'Psychological and psychiatric perspectives', in J. Fionda (ed.) *Legal concepts of childhood*, Oxford: Hart Publishers, pp 57-76.

Stainton Rogers, R. and Stainton Rogers, W. (1992) *Stories of childhood: Shifting agendas of child concern*, London: Harvester Wheatsheaf.

Stanley, K., Edwards, L. and Hatch, B. (2003) *The family report 2003: Choosing happiness?*, commissioned by Lever Faberge. London: IPPR.

Stenson, K. (2005) 'Sovereignty, biopolitics and the local government of crime in Britain', *Theoretical Criminology*, vol 9, no 3, pp 265-87.

Tomison, A.M. (2001) 'A history of child protection: back to the future?', *Family Matters*, no 60, pp 46-57.

Whittaker, J., Kenworthy, J. and Crabtree, C. (1998) *What children say about school*, Bolton Data for Inclusion, No 24, Bolton Institute of Higher Education.

Willow, C. (1999) *It's not fair*, London: The Children's Society.

Willow, C., Marchant, R., Kirby, P. and Neale, B. (2003) *Citizenship for young children: Strategies for development*, York: Joseph Rowntree Foundation.

Wood, M. (2004) *Perceptions and experience of antisocial behaviour: Findings from the 2003/2004 British Crime Survey*, London: Home Office.

Zipes, J. (2001) *Sticks and stones: The troublesome success of children's literature from Slovenly Peter to Harry Potter*, London: Routledge.

Index

B

babies 12
baby-sitting 16, 36, 46, 47
bargaining 53
bedtimes 52, 53
behaviour 33, 61, 64, 72, 118, 133, 141-4, 152
biological childhood 9
birth control 75
Blake, William 9
BMRB, *see* British Market Research Bureau
boomerang children 49
boundaries 9-10, 39, 47, 139
British Airways 104
British Child Study Association 61
British Crime Survey 142
British Gas study 50
British Market Research Bureau (BMRB) 21
BT and ChildLine study 81, 93
BT Openworld study 50
Bulger, James 5, 62
bullying 30, 36, 93

C

can-do attitude 91
capacity 44-5, 151
CAPI, *see* Computer-assisted Personal Interviewing
careers 29, 34, 54-6, 62, 98, 99
carers 72, 88, 90
celebrations 139
Census 21
chastisement, reasonable 66
child abuse, *see* abuse
child development, *see* development
child friendliness 1, 15, 21, 103-24, 128, 150-1
Child Friendly Communities Programme 105
childhood
  accounts of 3
  as a journey 9
  as a social category 2
  as a social construction 1, 7, 63
  attitudes to 60
  best things about 16, 31-4
  biological and social 9
  boundaries with adulthood 9-10, 39, 47
  definitions of 40-1
  disappearance of 9, 49

distinguished from adulthood 7-11
experience of 27-38
happy 16, 17, 27-9, 33, 37, 130, 137
idealisation of 8
images of 11-14
meaning of 1, 11, 148
natural 48
perceptions of 1-14
public presentation of 143-5
strict 16, 67, 68, 72
unhappy 28
worst things about 16, 34-7
Childhood Society 61
child labour 118
child offenders
child parents 14
child protection 134
child-rearing (childcare) manuals 59, 60, 75, 89
Children (Leaving Care) Act 41
Children (Protection at Work) (No 2) Regulations 44
Children Act (1908) 41
Children Act (1948) 6
Children Act (1989) 41, 76, 81
Children Act (2004) 41, 105, 151
children and young people strategy 105
Children and Young People's Unit (CYPU) 67, 81, 125
Children and Young Persons Act (1933) 40, 44, 46
Children and Young Persons Act (1963) 6
Children and Young Persons Act (1969) 6
Children of the Nineties 40
children
  as an asset 75
  as social actors 2, 45, 143
  as social group 2
  contact with 21, 87-90, 100
  influences on 16, 59-73, 147
  ownership of 76
  relationship with parents 76, 87, 147
  sale of 75
Children's Certificates 43
children's commissioners 81, 105, 151
child study 48, 61
child study associations 61
citizenship 6, 125, 137, 142, 143, 149, 152
citizenship curriculum 142, 145
clubs 36, 113, 117
communication 1, 93-6, 100, 134
competence 44-6, 76, 80, 130
compulsory schooling 42

Also available from The Policy Press

Families and the state: Two-way support and responsibilities

An inquiry into the relationship between the state and the family in the upbringing of children

Commission on Families and the Wellbeing of Children

Although outcomes for most children are good, the psychosocial problems for children in the UK remain worryingly high, with particular concerns existing over child poverty, disparities in health and education outcomes and young people's mental health. This report from The Commission on Families and the Wellbeing of Children addresses these critical issues in the context of the relationship between the state and the family. It considers ways in which the state should support families in their caring responsibilities and the difficult balance to be struck between the caring and control functions of the state in family governance.

Paperback £12.95 US$25.95 ISBN 1 86134 801 0

297 x 210mm 136 pages October 2005

A new deal for children?

Re-forming education and care in England, Scotland and Sweden

Bronwen Cohen, Peter Moss, Pat Petrie and Jennifer Wallace

"This is a fascinating study - an essential read for anyone seriously interested in reforming early years education." *David Hawker, Department of Children, Families and Schools, Brighton and Hove City Council*

"... a thought provoking, informed and instructive account, and an important point of reference for those who wish an analytic grip of many of the new concepts of governance around child care. Well worth reading whether you are an academic, policy maker, practitioner, student or anyone else interested in child care policies." *Journal of Social Policy*

Important reforms are taking place in children's services in the UK, with a move towards greater integration. In England, Scotland and Sweden, early childhood education and care, childcare for older children, and schools are now the responsibility of education departments. This book is the first to examine, cross-nationally, this major shift in policy.

Paperback £19.99 US$35.00 ISBN 1 86134 528 3

234 x 156mm 256 pages June 2004

Child welfare and social policy
An essential reader
Edited by Harry Hendrick

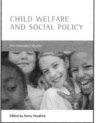

"This groundbreaking selection of seminal writings puts the subject of children and social policy in 21st-century Britain firmly on the map. Immense value is added by Harry Hendrick's introduction and trenchant critique, which locates every contribution within its specific policy context. This book is bound to become required reading for any under- and postgraduate social science student in the UK." *Eva Lloyd, Senior Lecturer in Early Childhood Studies, School for Policy Studies, University of Bristol*

"... invaluable reading for students and academics, as well as interesting and useful for health and social work professionals." *ChildRight*

This book provides an essential one-stop introduction to the key concepts, issues, policies and practices affecting child welfare, with particular emphasis on the changing nature of the relationship between child welfare and social policy. No other book brings together such a wide selection of material to form an attractive and indispensable teaching and learning resource.

Paperback £25.00 US$39.95 ISBN 1 86134 566 6
Hardback £55.00 US$85.00 ISBN 1 86134 567 4
240 x 172mm 576 pages March 2005

Child welfare
Historical dimensions, contemporary debate
Harry Hendrick

"Hendrick has provided us with a book to be appreciated and savoured, one offering students and the general reader a shrewd and intelligent overview of child welfare policy. Here is a standard text, one unlikely to be bettered for a long time." *Youth & Policy*

This book offers a provocative account of contemporary policies on child welfare and the ideological thrust behind them and provides an informed historical perspective on the evolution of child welfare during the last century.

Paperback £18.99 US$29.95 ISBN 1 86134 477 5
234 x 156mm 304 pages February 2003

Beyond listening

Children's perspectives on early childhood services

Edited by Alison Clark, Anne Trine Kjørholt and Peter Moss

This book is the first of its kind to focus on listening to young children, both from an international perspective and through combining theory, practice and reflection. With contributions and examples from researchers and practitioners in six countries it examines critically how listening to young children in early childhood services is understood and practiced.

Paperback £17.99 US$29.95 ISBN 1 86134 612 3

Hardback £50.00 US$75.00 ISBN 1 86134 613 1

240 x 172mm 208 pages October 2005

Children of the 21st century

From birth to nine months

Edited by Shirley Dex and Heather Joshi

This book documents the early lives of almost 19,000 children born in the UK at the start of the 21st century, and their families. It is the first time that analysis of data from the hugely important Millennium Cohort Study, a longitudinal study following the progress of the children and their families, has been drawn together in a single volume. The unrivalled data is examined here to address important policy and scientific issues.

Paperback £24.99 US$39.95 ISBN 1 86134 688 3

Hardback £55.00 US$85.00 ISBN 1 86134 689 1

234 x 156mm 296 pages October 2005

The UK Millennium Cohort Study series

To order copies of these publications or any other Policy Press titles please visit **www.policypress.org.uk** or contact:

In the UK and Europe:
Marston Book Services, PO Box 269,
Abingdon, Oxon, OX14 4YN, UK
Tel: +44 (0)1235 465500
Fax: +44 (0)1235 465556
Email: direct.orders@marston.co.uk

In the USA and Canada:
ISBS, 920 NE 58th Street, Suite 300,
Portland, OR 97213-3786, USA
Tel: +1 800 944 6190 (toll free)
Fax: +1 503 280 8832
Email: info@isbs.com

In Australia and New Zealand:
DA Information Services, 648 Whitehorse Road
Mitcham, Victoria 3132, Australia
Tel: +61 (3) 9210 7777
Fax: +61 (3) 9210 7788
E-mail: service@dadirect.com.au